LIGHT ON THE PATH

THROUGH THE GATES OF GOLD

THE present edition of LIGHT ON THE PATH is a verbatim reprint of the 1888 edition (George Redway, London) in which later edition the NOTES by the Author first appear. The COMMENTS, which are not in the 1888 edition, are here taken directly from *Lucifer,* Volume I, 1887-8, where they were first published.

Also in this volume we reprint verbatim the original edition (1887) of THROUGH THE GATES OF GOLD by the same Author, together with a commentary by William Q. Judge taken from his magazine, *The Path,* March, 1887.

Light on the Path

A Treatise

WRITTEN FOR THE PERSONAL USE OF THOSE WHO
ARE IGNORANT OF THE EASTERN WISDOM, AND
WHO DESIRE TO ENTER WITHIN ITS INFLUENCE

Written down by M. C.
with Notes by the Author

THEOSOPHICAL UNIVERSITY PRESS
PASADENA, CALIFORNIA

Theosophical University Press
Post Office Box C
Pasadena, California 91109-7107
1997

The paper in this book is acid-free and meets the standards for
permanence of the Council on Library Resources.

Library of Congress Catalog Card Number 68-21157

ISBN 0-911500-37-5   cloth
ISBN 0-911500-38-3 softcover

Printed at Theosophical University Press
Pasadena, California

LIGHT ON THE PATH

LIGHT ON THE PATH

I

THESE rules are written for all disciples: Attend you to them.

Before the eyes can see, they must be incapable of tears. Before the ear can hear, it must have lost its sensitiveness. Before the voice can speak in the presence of the Masters it must have lost the power to wound. Before the soul can stand in the presence of the Masters its feet must be washed in the blood of the heart.

1. Kill out ambition.

2. Kill out desire of life.

3. Kill out desire of comfort.

4. Work as those work who are ambitious.

Respect life as those do who desire it. Be happy as those are who live for happiness.

Seek in the heart the source of evil and expunge it. It lives fruitfully in the heart of the devoted disciple as well as in the heart of the man of desire. Only the strong can kill it out. The weak must wait for its growth, its fruition, its death. And it is a plant that lives and increases throughout the ages. It flowers when the man has accumulated unto himself innumerable existences. He who will enter upon the path of power must tear this thing out of his heart. And then the heart will bleed, and the whole life of the man seem to be utterly dissolved. This ordeal must be endured: it may come at the first step of the perilous ladder which leads to the path of life: it may not come until the last. But, O disciple, remember that it has to be endured, and fasten the energies of your soul upon the task. Live neither in the present nor the future, but in the eternal. This giant weed cannot flower there: this blot upon existence is wiped out by the very atmosphere of eternal thought.

[2]

5. Kill out all sense of separateness.

6. Kill out desire for sensation.

7. Kill out the hunger for growth.

8. Yet stand alone and isolated, because nothing that is imbodied, nothing that is conscious of separation, nothing that is out of the eternal, can aid you. Learn from sensation and observe it, because only so can you commence the science of self-knowledge, and plant your foot on the first step of the ladder. Grow as the flower grows, unconsciously, but eagerly anxious to open its soul to the air. So must you press forward to open your soul to the eternal. But it must be the eternal that draws forth your strength and beauty, not desire of growth. For in the one case you develop in the luxuriance of purity, in the other you harden by the forcible passion for personal stature.

9. Desire only that which is within you.

10. Desire only that which is beyond you.

11. Desire only that which is unattainable.

[3]

12. For within you is the light of the world — the only light that can be shed upon the Path. If you are unable to perceive it within you, it is useless to look for it elsewhere. It is beyond you; because when you reach it you have lost yourself. It is unattainable, because it for ever recedes. You will enter the light, but you will never touch the flame.

13. Desire power ardently.

14. Desire peace fervently.

15. Desire possessions above all.

16. But those possessions must belong to the pure soul only, and be possessed therefore by all pure souls equally, and thus be the especial property of the whole only when united. Hunger for such possessions as can be held by the pure soul, that you may accumulate wealth for that united spirit of life which is your only true self. The peace you shall desire is that sacred peace which nothing can disturb, and in which the soul grows as does the holy flower upon the still lagoons. And that power

which the disciple shall covet is that which shall make him appear as nothing in the eyes of men.

17. Seek out the way.

18. Seek the way by retreating within.

19. Seek the way by advancing boldly without.

20. Seek it not by any one road. To each temperament there is one road which seems the most desirable. But the way is not found by devotion alone, by religious contemplation alone, by ardent progress, by self-sacrificing labor, by studious observation of life. None alone can take the disciple more than one step onward. All steps are necessary to make up the ladder. The vices of men become steps in the ladder, one by one, as they are surmounted. The virtues of man are steps indeed, necessary — not by any means to be dispensed with. Yet, though they create a fair atmosphere and a happy future, they are useless if they stand alone. The whole nature of man must be used

wisely by the one who desires to enter the way.
Each man is to himself absolutely the way, the
truth, and the life. But he is only so when he
grasps his whole individuality firmly, and, by
the force of his awakened spiritual will, recognizes this individuality as not himself, but that
thing which he has with pain created for his
own use, and by means of which he purposes,
as his growth slowly develops his intelligence,
to reach to the life beyond individuality. When
he knows that for this his wonderful complex
separated life exists, then, indeed, and then
only, he is upon the way. Seek it by plunging
into the mysterious and glorious depths of your
own inmost being. Seek it by testing all experience, by utilizing the senses in order to
understand the growth and meaning of individuality, and the beauty and obscurity of those
other divine fragments which are struggling
side by side with you, and form the race to
which you belong. Seek it by study of the laws
of being, the laws of nature, the laws of the
supernatural: and seek it by making the profound obeisance of the soul to the dim star that

burns within. Steadily, as you watch and wor-
ship, its light will grow stronger. Then you
may know you have found the beginning of
the way. And when you have found the end its
light will suddenly become the infinite light.

21. Look for the flower to bloom in the
silence that follows the storm: not till then.

It shall grow, it will shoot up, it will make
branches and leaves and form buds, while the
storm continues, while the battle lasts. But
not till the whole personality of the man is dissolved and melted — not until it is held by the
divine fragment which has created it, as a mere
subject for grave experiment and experience —
not until the whole nature has yielded and
become subject unto its higher self, can the
bloom open. Then will come a calm such as
comes in a tropical country after the heavy rain,
when Nature works so swiftly that one may see
her action. Such a calm will come to the ha-
rassed spirit. And in the deep silence the mysterious event will occur which will prove that
the way has been found. Call it by what name

you will, it is a voice that speaks where there is none to speak — it is a messenger that comes, a messenger without form or substance; or it is the flower of the soul that has opened. It cannot be described by any metaphor. But it can be felt after, looked for, and desired, even amid the raging of the storm. The silence may last a moment of time or it may last a thousand years. But it will end. Yet you will carry its strength with you. Again and again the battle must be fought and won. It is only for an interval that Nature can be still.

These written above are the first of the rules which are written on the walls of the Hall of Learning. Those that ask shall have. Those that desire to read shall read. Those who desire to learn shall learn.

PEACE BE WITH YOU.

△

II

OUT of the silence that is peace a resonant voice shall arise. And this voice will say, It is not well; thou hast reaped, now thou must sow. And knowing this voice to be the silence itself thou wilt obey.

Thou who art now a disciple, able to stand, able to hear, able to see, able to speak, who hast conquered desire and attained to self-knowledge, who hast seen thy soul in its bloom and recognized it, and heard the voice of the silence, go thou to the Hall of Learning and read what is written there for thee.

1. Stand aside in the coming battle, and though thou fightest be not thou the warrior.

2. Look for the warrior and let him fight in thee.

3. Take his orders for battle and obey them.

4. Obey him not as though he were a gen-

eral, but as though he were thyself, and his spoken words were the utterance of thy secret desires; for he is thyself, yet infinitely wiser and stronger than thyself. Look for him, else in the fever and hurry of the fight thou mayest pass him; and he will not know thee unless thou knowest him. If thy cry meet his listening ear, then will he fight in thee and fill the dull void within. And if this is so, then canst thou go through the fight cool and unwearied, standing aside and letting him battle for thee. Then it will be impossible for thee to strike one blow amiss. But if thou look not for him, if thou pass him by, then there is no safeguard for thee. Thy brain will reel, thy heart grow uncertain, and in the dust of the battlefield thy sight and senses will fail, and thou wilt not know thy friends from thy enemies.

He is thyself, yet thou art but finite and liable to error. He is eternal and is sure. He is eternal truth. When once he has entered thee and become thy warrior, he will never utterly desert thee, and at the day of the great peace he will become one with thee.

5. Listen to the song of life.

6. Store in your memory the melody you hear.

7. Learn from it the lesson of harmony.

8. You can stand upright now, firm as a rock amid the turmoil, obeying the warrior who is thyself and thy king. Unconcerned in the battle save to do his bidding, having no longer any care as to the result of the battle, for one thing only is important, that the warrior shall win, and you know he is incapable of defeat — standing thus, cool and awakened, use the hearing you have acquired by pain and by the destruction of pain. Only fragments of the great song come to your ears while yet you are but man. But if you listen to it, remember it faithfully, so that none which has reached you is lost, and endeavor to learn from it the meaning of the mystery which surrounds you. In time you will need no teacher. For as the individual has voice, so has that in which the individual exists. Life itself has speech and is

never silent. And its utterance is not, as you that are deaf may suppose, a cry: it is a song. Learn from it that you are part of the harmony; learn from it to obey the laws of the harmony.

9. Regard earnestly all the life that surrounds you.

10. Learn to look intelligently into the hearts of men.

11. Regard most earnestly your own heart.

12. For through your own heart comes the one light which can illuminate life and make it clear to your eyes.

Study the hearts of men, that you may know what is that world in which you live and of which you will to be a part. Regard the constantly changing and moving life which surrounds you, for it is formed by the hearts of men; and as you learn to understand their constitution and meaning, you will by degrees be able to read the larger word of life.

13. Speech comes only with knowledge. Attain to knowledge and you will attain to speech.

14. Having obtained the use of the inner senses, having conquered the desires of the outer senses, having conquered the desires of the individual soul, and having obtained knowledge, prepare now, O disciple, to enter upon the way in reality. The path is found: make yourself ready to tread it.

15. Inquire of the earth, the air, and the water, of the secrets they hold for you. The development of your inner senses will enable you to do this.

16. Inquire of the holy ones of the earth of the secrets they hold for you. The conquering of the desires of the outer senses will give you the right to do this.

17. Inquire of the inmost, the one, of its final secret which it holds for you through the ages.

The great and difficult victory, the conquering of the desires of the individual soul, is a work of ages; therefore expect not to obtain its reward until ages of experience have been accumulated. When the time of learning this seventeenth rule is reached, man is on the threshold of becoming more than man.

18. The knowledge which is now yours is only yours because your soul has become one with all pure souls and with the inmost. It is a trust vested in you by the Most High. Betray it, misuse your knowledge, or neglect it, and it is possible even now for you to fall from the high estate you have attained. Great ones fall back, even from the threshold, unable to sustain the weight of their responsibility, unable to pass on. Therefore look forward always with awe and trembling to this moment, and be prepared for the battle.

19. It is written that for him who is on the threshold of divinity no law can be framed, no guide can exist. Yet to enlighten the disciple, the final struggle may be thus expressed:

[14]

Hold fast to that which has neither substance nor existence.

20. Listen only to the voice which is soundless.

21. Look only on that which is invisible alike to the inner and the outer sense.

PEACE BE WITH YOU.

△

NOTES

Note on Rule 1. — Ambition is the first curse: the great tempter of the man who is rising above his fellows. It is the simplest form of looking for reward. Men of intelligence and power are led away from their higher possibilities by it continually. Yet it is a necessary teacher. Its results turn to dust and ashes in the mouth; like death and estrangement it shows the man at last that to work for self is to work for disappointment. But though this first rule seems so simple and easy, do not quickly pass it by. For these vices of the ordinary man pass through a subtle transformation and reappear with changed aspect in the heart of the disciple. It is easy to say, I will not be ambitious: it is not so easy to say, when the Master reads my heart he will find it clean utterly. The pure artist who works for the love of his work is sometimes more firmly planted on the right road than the occultist, who fancies he has removed his interest from self, but who has in reality only enlarged the limits of experience and desire, and transferred his interest to the things which concern his larger span of life. The same principle applies to the other two seemingly simple rules. Linger over them and do not let yourself be easily deceived by your own heart. For now, at the threshold, a mistake can be corrected. But carry it on with you and it will grow and come to fruition, or else you must suffer bitterly in its destruction.

Note on Rule 5. — Do not fancy you can stand aside from the bad man or the foolish man. They are yourself, though in a less degree than your friend or your master. But if you allow the idea of separateness from any evil thing or person to grow up within you, by so doing you create Karma, which will bind you to that thing or person till your soul recognizes that it cannot be isolated. Remember that the sin and shame of the world are your sin and shame; for you are a part of it;

[18]

your Karma is inextricably interwoven with the great Karma. And before you can attain knowledge you must have passed through all places, foul and clean alike. Therefore, remember that the soiled garment you shrink from touching may have been yours yesterday, may be yours tomorrow. And if you turn with horror from it, when it is flung upon your shoulders, it will cling the more closely to you. The self-righteous man makes for himself a bed of mire. Abstain because it is right to abstain — not that yourself shall be kept clean.

Note on Rule 17. — These four words seem, perhaps, too slight to stand alone. The disciple may say, Should I study these thoughts at all did I not seek out the way? Yet do not pass on hastily. Pause and consider awhile. Is it the way you desire, or is it that there is a dim perspective in your visions of great heights to be scaled by yourself, of a great future for you to compass? Be warned. The way is to be sought for its own sake, not with regard to your feet that shall tread it.

There is a correspondence between this rule and the 17th of the 2nd series. When after ages of struggle and many victories the final battle is won, the final secret demanded, then you are prepared for a further path. When the final secret of this great lesson is told, in it is opened the mystery of the new way — a path which leads out of all human experience, and which is utterly beyond human perception or imagination. At each of these points it is needful to pause long and consider well. At each of these points it is necessary to be sure that the way is chosen for its own sake. The way and the truth come first, then follows the life.

Note on Rule 20. — Seek it by testing all experience, and remember that when I say this I do not say, Yield to the seductions of sense in order to know it. Before you have become an occultist you may do this; but not afterwards. When you have chosen and entered the path you cannot yield to these seductions without shame. Yet you can experience them without horror: can weigh, observe and test them, and wait with the patience of confidence for the hour when they shall affect you no longer. But do not condemn the man that yields; stretch out your hand to him as a brother pilgrim whose feet have become heavy with mire. Remember, O disciple, that great though the gulf may be between the good man and the sinner, it is greater between the good man and the man who has attained knowledge; it is immeasurable between the good man and the one on the threshold of divinity. Therefore be wary lest too soon you fancy yourself a thing apart from the mass. When you have found the beginning of the way the star of your soul will show its light; and by that light you will perceive how great is the darkness in which it burns. Mind, heart, brain, all are obscure and dark until the first great battle has been won. Be not appalled and terrified by this sight; keep your eyes fixed on the small light and it will grow. But let the darkness

[21]

within help you to understand the helplessness of those who have seen no light, whose souls are in profound gloom. Blame them not, shrink not from them, but try to lift a little of the heavy Karma of the world; give your aid to the few strong hands that hold back the powers of darkness from obtaining complete victory. Then do you enter into a partnership of joy, which brings indeed terrible toil and profound sadness, but also a great and ever-increasing delight.

Note on Rule 21. — The opening of the bloom is the glorious moment when perception awakes: with it comes confidence, knowledge, certainty. The pause of the soul is the moment of wonder, and the next moment of satisfaction, that is the silence.

Know, O disciple, that those who have passed through the silence, and felt its peace and retained its strength, they long that you shall pass through it also. Therefore, in the Hall of Learning, when he is capable of enter-

[22]

ing there, the disciple will always find his master.

Those that ask shall have. But though the ordinary man asks perpetually, his voice is not heard. For he asks with his mind only; and the voice of the mind is only heard on that plane on which the mind acts. Therefore, not until the first twenty-one rules are past do I say those that ask shall have.

To read, in the occult sense, is to read with the eyes of the spirit. To ask is to feel the hunger within — the yearning of spiritual aspiration. To be able to read means having obtained the power in a small degree of gratifying that hunger. When the disciple is ready to learn, then he is accepted, acknowledged, recognized. It must be so, for he has lit his lamp, and it cannot be hidden. But to learn is impossible until the first great battle has been won. The mind may recognize truth, but the spirit cannot receive it. Once having passed through the storm and attained the peace, it is then always possible to learn, even though the disciple waver, hesitate, and turn aside. The voice of the silence remains within him, and though he leave the path utterly, yet one day it will resound and rend him asunder and separate his passions from his divine possibilities. Then with pain and desperate cries from the deserted lower self he will return.

Therefore I say, Peace be with you. My peace I give unto you can only be said by the Master to the beloved disciples who are as himself. There are some even among those who are ignorant of the Eastern wisdom to whom this can be said, and to whom it can daily be said with more completeness.

△ Regard the three truths. They are equal.

Part II

Note on Sect. II — To be able to stand is to have confidence; to be able to hear is to have opened the doors of the soul; to be able to see is to have attained perception; to be able to speak is to have attained the power of helping others; to have conquered desire

[24]

is to have learned how to use and control the self; to have attained to self-knowledge is to have retreated to the inner fortress from whence the personal man can be viewed with impartiality; to have seen thy soul in its bloom is to have obtained a momentary glimpse in thyself of the transfiguration which shall eventually make thee more than man; to recognize is to achieve the great task of gazing upon the blazing light without dropping the eyes and not falling back in terror, as though before some ghastly phantom. This happens to some, and so when the victory is all but won it is lost; to hear the voice of the silence is to understand that from within comes the only true guidance; to go to the Hall of Learning is to enter the state in which learning becomes possible. Then will many words be written there for thee, and written in fiery letters for thee easily to read. For when the disciple is ready the Master is ready also.

Note on Rule 5. — Look for it and listen to it first in your own heart. At first you may

say it is not there; when I search I find only
discord. Look deeper. If again you are dis-
appointed, pause and look deeper again. There
is a natural melody, an obscure fount in every
human heart. It may be hidden over and utterly concealed and silenced — but it is there.
At the very base of your nature you will find
faith, hope, and love. He that chooses evil
refuses to look within himself, shuts his ears to
the melody of his heart, as he blinds his eyes
to the light of his soul. He does this because
he finds it easier to live in desires. But under-
neath all life is the strong current that cannot
be checked; the great waters are there in reality. Find them, and you will perceive that none,
not the most wretched of creatures, but is a
part of it, however he blind himself to the
fact and build up for himself a phantasmal
outer form of horror. In that sense it is that I
say to you — All those beings among whom
you struggle on are fragments of the Divine.
And so deceptive is the illusion in which you
live, that it is hard to guess where you will first
detect the sweet voice in the hearts of others.

But know that it is certainly within yourself. Look for it there, and once having heard it, you will more readily recognize it around you.

Note on Rule 10. — From an absolutely impersonal point of view, otherwise your sight is colored. Therefore impersonality must first be understood.

Intelligence is impartial: no man is your enemy: no man is your friend. All alike are your teachers. Your enemy becomes a mystery that must be solved, even though it take ages: for man must be understood. Your friend becomes a part of yourself, an extension of yourself, a riddle hard to read. Only one thing is more difficult to know — your own heart. Not until the bonds of personality are loosed, can that profound mystery of self begin to be seen. Not till you stand aside from it will it in any way reveal itself to your understanding. Then, and not till then, can you grasp and guide it. Then, and not till then, can you use all its powers, and devote them to a worthy service.

[27]

Note on Rule 13. — It is impossible to help others till you have obtained some certainty of your own. When you have learned the first 21 rules and have entered the Hall of Learning with your powers developed and sense unchained, then you will find there is a fount within you from which speech will arise.

After the 13th rule I can add no words to what is already written.

My peace I give unto you.   △

These notes are written only for those to whom I give my peace; those who can read what I have written with the inner as well as the outer sense.

COMMENTS

I

"BEFORE THE EYES CAN SEE THEY MUST BE
INCAPABLE OF TEARS."

IT should be very clearly remembered by
all readers of this volume that it is a book
which may appear to have some little philosophy in it, but very little sense, to those who
believe it to be written in ordinary English.
To the many, who read in this manner it will
be — not caviare so much as olives strong of
their salt. Be warned and read but a little in
this way.

There is another way of reading, which is,
indeed, the only one of any use with many
authors. It is reading, not between the lines
but within the words. In fact, it is decipher-
ing a profound cipher. All alchemical works
are written in the cipher of which I speak;

it has been used by the great philosophers and poets of all time. It is used systematically by the adepts in life and knowledge, who, seemingly giving out their deepest wisdom, hide in the very words which frame it its actual mystery. They cannot do more. There is a law of nature which insists that a man shall read these mysteries for himself. By no other method can he obtain them. A man who desires to live must eat his food himself: this is the simple law of nature — which applies also to the higher life. A man who would live and act in it cannot be fed like a babe with a spoon; he must eat for himself.

I propose to put into new and sometimes plainer language parts of "Light on the Path"; but whether this effort of mine will really be any interpretation I cannot say. To a deaf and dumb man, a truth is made no more intelligible if, in order to make it so, some misguided linguist translates the words in which it is couched into every living or dead language, and shouts these different phrases in his ear. But for those who are not deaf and dumb one language is generally easier than the rest; and it is to such as these I address myself.

The very first aphorisms of "Light on the Path," included under Number I. have, I know well, remained sealed as to their inner meaning to many who have otherwise followed the purpose of the book.

There are four proven and certain truths with regard to the entrance to occultism. The Gates of Gold bar that threshold; yet there are some who pass those gates and discover the sublime and illimitable beyond. In the far spaces of Time all will pass those gates. But I am one who wish that Time, the great deluder, were not so over-masterful. To those who know and love him I have no word to say; but to the others — and there are not so very few as some may fancy — to whom the passage of Time is as the stroke of a sledge-hammer, and the sense of Space like the bars of an iron cage, I will translate and re-translate until they understand fully.

The four truths written on the first page of "Light on the Path," refer to the trial in-

itiation of the would-be occultist. Until he has
passed it, he cannot even reach to the latch of
the gate which admits to knowledge. Knowledge is man's greatest inheritance; why, then,
should he not attempt to reach it by every
possible road? The laboratory is not the only
ground for experiment; *science,* we must remember, is derived from *sciens,* present parti-
ciple of *scire,* "to know," — its origin is similar to that of the word "discern," "to ken."
Science does not therefore deal only with
matter, no, not even its subtlest and obscurest
forms. Such an idea is born merely of the idle
spirit of the age. Science is a word which
covers all forms of knowledge. It is exceed-
ingly interesting to hear what chemists discover,
and to see them finding their way through the
densities of matter to its finer forms; but there
are other kinds of knowledge than this, and it
is not every one who restricts his (strictly scientific) desire for knowledge to experiments
which are capable of being tested by the physical senses.

Everyone who is not a dullard, or a man

stupefied by some predominant vice, has guessed, or even perhaps discovered with some certainty, that there are subtle senses lying within the physical senses. There is nothing at all extraordinary in this; if we took the trouble to call Nature into the witness box we should find that everything which is perceptible to the ordinary sight, has something even more important than itself hidden within it; the microscope has opened a world to us, but within those encasements which the microscope reveals, lies a mystery which no machinery can probe.

The whole world is animated and lit, down to its most material shapes, by a world within it. This inner world is called Astral by some people, and it is as good a word as any other, though it merely means starry; but the stars, as Locke pointed out, are luminous bodies which give light of themselves. This quality is characteristic of the life which lies within matter; for those who see it, need no lamp to see it by. The word star, moreover, is derived from the Anglo-Saxon "stir-an," to steer, to stir, to move, and undeniably it is the inner life which is master of the outer, just as a man's brain guides the movements of his lips. So that although Astral is no very excellent word in itself, I am content to use it for my present purpose.

The whole of "Light on the Path" is written in an astral cipher and can therefore only be deciphered by one who reads astrally. And its teaching is chiefly directed towards the cultivation and development of the astral life. Until the first step has been taken in this development, the swift knowledge, which is called intuition with certainty, is impossible to man. And this positive and certain intuition is the only form of knowledge which enables a man to work rapidly or reach his true and high estate, within the limit of his conscious effort. To obtain knowledge by experiment is too tedious a method for those who aspire to accomplish real work; he who gets it by certain intuition, lays hands on its various forms with supreme rapidity, by fierce effort of will; as a determined workman grasps his tools, indifferent to their weight or any other difficulty which may stand in his way. He does not stay for each to be tested — he uses such as he sees are fittest.

All the rules contained in "Light on the Path," are written for all disciples, but only for disciples — those who "take knowledge." To none else but the student in this school are its laws of any use or interest.

To all who are interested seriously in Occultism, I say first — take knowledge. To him who hath shall be given. It is useless to wait for it. The womb of Time will close before you, and in later days you will remain unborn, without power. I therefore say to those who have any hunger or thirst for knowledge, attend to these rules.

They are none of my handicraft or invention. They are merely the phrasing of laws in super-nature, the putting into words truths as absolute in their own sphere, as those laws which govern the conduct of the earth and its atmosphere.

[35]

The senses spoken of in these four statements are the astral, or inner senses.

No man desires to see that light which illumines the spaceless soul until pain and sorrow and despair have driven him away from the life of ordinary humanity. First he wears out pleasure; then he wears out pain — till, at last, his eyes become incapable of tears.

This is a truism, although I know perfectly well that it will meet with a vehement denial from many who are in sympathy with thoughts which spring from the inner life. *To see* with the astral sense of sight is a form of activity which it is difficult for us to understand immediately. The scientist knows very well what a miracle is achieved by each child that is born into the world, when it first conquers its eyesight and compels it to obey its brain. An equal miracle is performed with each sense certainly, but this ordering of sight is perhaps the most stupendous effort. Yet the child does it almost unconsciously, by force of the powerful heredity of habit. No one now is aware that he has ever done it at all; just as we cannot recollect the individual movements which enabled us to walk up a hill a year ago. This arises from the fact that we move and live and have our being in matter. Our knowledge of it has become intuitive.

With our astral life it is very much otherwise. For long ages past, man has paid very little attention to it — so little, that he has practically lost the use of his senses. It is true, that in every civilization the star arises, and man confesses, with more or less of folly and confusion, that he knows himself to be. But most often he denies it, and in being a materialist becomes that strange thing, a being which cannot see its own light, a thing of life which will not live, an astral animal which has eyes, and ears, and speech, and power, yet will use none of these gifts. This is the case, and the habit of ignorance has become so confirmed, that now none will see with the inner vision till agony has made the physical eyes not only unseeing, but without tears — the moisture of life. To be incapable of tears is to have faced and conquered the simple human nature, and to have attained an equilibrium which cannot be shaken by personal emotions. It does not imply any hardness of heart, or any indifference. It does not imply the exhaustion of sorrow, when the suffering soul seems powerless to suffer acutely any longer; it does not mean the deadness of old age, when emotion is becoming dull because the strings which vibrate to it are wearing out. None of these conditions are fit for a disciple, and if any one of them exist in him it must be overcome before the path can be entered upon. Hardness of heart belongs to the selfish man, the egotist, to whom the gate is for ever closed. Indifference belongs to the fool and the false philosopher; those whose lukewarmness makes them mere puppets, not strong enough to face the realities of existence. When pain or sorrow has worn out the keenness of suffering, the result is a lethargy not unlike that which accompanies old age, as it is usually experienced by men and women. Such a condition makes the entrance to the path impossible, because the first step is one of difficulty and needs a strong man, full

[38]

of psychic and physical vigor, to attempt it.

It is a truth, that, as Edgar Allan Poe said, the eyes are the windows for the soul, the windows of that haunted palace in which it dwells. This is the very nearest interpretation into ordinary language of the meaning of the text. If grief, dismay, disappointment or pleasure, can shake the soul so that it loses its fixed hold on the calm spirit which inspires it, and the moisture of life breaks forth, drowning knowledge in sensation, then all is blurred, the windows are darkened, the light is useless. This is as literal a fact as that if a man, at the edge of a precipice, loses his nerve through some sudden emotion he will certainly fall. The poise of the body, the balance, must be preserved, not only in dangerous places, but even on the level ground, and with all the assistance Nature gives us by the law of gravitation. So it is with the soul, it is the link between the outer body and the starry spirit beyond; the divine spark dwells in the still place where no convulsion of Nature can shake the air; this is so always. But the soul may lose its hold on that, its knowledge of it, even though these two are part of one whole; and it is by emotion, by sensation, that this hold is loosed. To suffer either pleasure or pain, causes a vivid vibration which is, to the consciousness of man, life. Now this sensibility does not lessen when the disciple enters upon his training; it increases. It is the first test of his strength; he must suffer, must enjoy or endure, more keenly than other men, while yet he has taken on him a duty which does not exist for other men, that of not allowing his suffering to shake him from his fixed purpose. He has, in fact, at the first step to take himself steadily in hand and put the bit into his own mouth; no one else can do it for him.

The first four aphorisms of "Light on the Path," refer entirely to astral development. This development must be accomplished to a certain extent — that is to say it must be fully entered upon — before the remainder of the book is really intelligible except to the intellect; in fact, before it can be read as a practical, not a metaphysical treatise.

In one of the great mystic Brotherhoods, there are four ceremonies, that take place early in the year, which practically illustrate and elucidate these aphorisms. They are ceremonies in which only novices take part, for they are simply services of the threshold. But it will show how serious a thing it is to become a disciple, when it is understood that these are all ceremonies of sacrifice. The first one is this of which I have been speaking. The keenest enjoyment, the bitterest pain, the anguish of loss and despair, are brought to bear on the trembling soul, which has not yet found light in the darkness, which is helpless as a blind man is, and until these shocks can be endured without loss of equilibrium the astral senses must remain sealed. This is the merciful law. The "medium," or "spiritualist," who rushes into the psychic world without preparation, is a law-breaker, a breaker of the laws of super-nature. Those who break Nature's laws lose their physical health; those who break the laws of the inner life, lose their psychic health. "Mediums" become mad, suicides, miserable creatures devoid of moral sense; and often end as unbelievers, doubters even of that which their own eyes have seen. The disciple is compelled to become his own master before he adventures on this perilous path, and attempts to face those beings who live and work in the astral world, and whom we call masters, because of their great knowledge and their ability to control not only themselves but the forces around them.

The condition of the soul when it lives for the life of sensation as distinguished from that of knowledge, is vibratory or oscillating, as distinguished from fixed. That is the nearest literal representation of the fact; but it is only literal to the intellect, not to the intuition. For this part of man's consciousness a different vocabulary is needed. The idea of "fixed" might perhaps be transposed into that of "at home." In sensation no permanent home can be found, because change is the law of this vibratory existence. That fact is the first one which must be learned by the disciple. It is useless to pause and weep for a scene in a kaleidoscope which has passed.

It is a very well-known fact, one with which Bulwer Lytton dealt with great power, that an intolerable sadness is the very first experience of the neophyte in Occultism. A sense of blankness falls upon him which makes the world a waste, and life a vain exertion. This follows his first serious contemplation of the abstract. In gazing, or even in attempting to gaze, on the ineffable mystery of his own higher nature, he himself causes the initial trial to fall on him. The oscillation between pleasure and pain ceases for — perhaps an instant of time; but that is enough to have cut him loose from his fast moorings in the world of sensation. He has experienced, however briefly, the greater life; and he goes on with ordinary existence weighted by a sense of unreality, of blank, of horrid negation. This was the nightmare which visited Bulwer Lytton's neophyte in "Zanoni"; and even Zanoni himself, who had learned great truths, and been entrusted with great powers, had not actually passed the threshold where fear and hope, despair and joy seem at one moment absolute realities, at the next mere forms of fancy.

This initial trial is often brought on us by life itself. For life is after all, the great teacher. We return to study it, after we have acquired power over it, just as the master in chemistry learns more in the laboratory than his pupil does. There are persons so near the door of knowledge that life itself prepares them for it, and no individual hand has to invoke the hideous guardian of the entrance. These must naturally be keen and powerful organizations, capable of the most vivid pleasure; then pain comes and fills its great duty. The most intense forms of suffering fall on such a nature, till at last it arouses from its stupor of consciousness, and by the force of its internal vitality steps over the threshold into a place of peace. Then the vibration of life loses its power of tyranny. The sensitive nature must suffer still; but the soul has freed itself and stands aloof, guiding the life towards its greatness. Those who are the subjects of Time, and go slowly through all his spaces, live on through a long-drawn series of sensations, and suffer a constant mingling of pleasure and of pain. They do not dare to take the snake of self in a steady grasp and conquer it, so becoming divine; but prefer to go on fretting through divers experiences, suffering blows from the opposing forces.

When one of these subjects of Time decides to enter on the path of Occultism, it is this which is his first task. If life has not taught it to him, if he is not strong enough to teach himself, and if he has power enough to demand the help of a master, then this fearful trial, depicted in Zanoni, is put upon him. The oscillation in which he lives, is for an instant stilled; and he has to survive the shock of facing what seems to him at first sight as the abyss of nothingness. Not till he has learned to dwell in this abyss, and has found its peace, is it possible for his eyes to have become incapable of tears.

△

II

"BEFORE THE EAR CAN HEAR, IT MUST
HAVE LOST ITS SENSITIVENESS."

The first four rules of "Light on the Path"
are, undoubtedly, curious though the statement
may seem, the most important in the whole
book, save one only. Why they are so important is that they contain the vital law, the very
creative essence of the astral man. And it is
only in the astral (or self-illuminated) consciousness that the rules which follow them
have any living meaning. Once attain to the
use of the astral senses and it becomes a matter
of course that one commences to use them;
and the later rules are but guidance in their
use. When I speak like this I mean, naturally,
that the first four rules are the ones which are
of importance and interest to those who read
them in print upon a page. When they are
engraved on a man's heart and on his life, un-
mistakably then the other rules become not

merely interesting, or extraordinary, meta-physical statements, but actual facts in life which have to be grasped and experienced.

The four rules stand written in the great chamber of every actual lodge of a living Brotherhood. Whether the man is about to sell his soul to the devil, like Faust; whether he is to be worsted in the battle, like Hamlet; or whether he is to pass on within the pre-cincts; in any case these words are for him. The man can choose between virtue and vice, but not until he is a man; a babe or a wild animal cannot so choose. Thus with the dis-ciple, he must first become a disciple before he can even see the paths to choose between. This effort of creating himself as a disciple, the re-birth, he must do for himself without any teacher. Until the four rules are learned no teacher can be of any use to him; and that is why "the Masters" are referred to in the way they are. No real masters, whether adepts in power, in love, or in blackness, can affect a man till these four rules are passed.

Tears, as I have said, may be called the

moisture of life. The soul must have laid aside
the emotions of humanity, must have secured
a balance which cannot be shaken by mis-
fortune, before its eyes can open upon the
super-human world.

The voice of the Masters is always in the
world; but only those hear it whose ears are
no longer receptive of the sounds which affect
the personal life. Laughter no longer lightens
the heart, anger may no longer enrage it, tender words bring it no balm. For that within,
to which the ears are as an outer gateway, is
an unshaken place of peace in itself which no
person can disturb.

As the eyes are the windows of the soul, so
are the ears its gateways or doors. Through
them comes knowledge of the confusion of the
world. The great ones who have conquered
life, who have become more than disciples,
stand at peace and undisturbed amid the
vibration and kaleidoscopic movement of
humanity. They hold within themselves a certain knowledge, as well as a perfect peace; and
thus they are not roused or excited by the

partial and erroneous fragments of information which are brought to their ears by the changing voices of those around them. When I speak of knowledge, I mean intuitive knowledge. This certain information can never be obtained by hard work, or by experiment; for these methods are only applicable to matter, and matter is in itself a perfectly uncertain substance, continually affected by change. The most absolute and universal laws of natural and physical life, as understood by the scientist, will pass away when the life of this universe has passed away, and only its soul is left in the silence. What then will be the value of the knowledge of its laws acquired by industry and observation? I pray that no reader or critic will imagine that by what I have said I intend to depreciate or disparage acquired knowledge, or the work of scientists. On the contrary, I hold that scientific men are the pioneers of modern thought. The days of literature and of art, when poets and sculptors saw the divine light, and put it into their own great language — these days lie buried in the long past with the ante-Phidian sculptors and the pre-Homeric poets. The mysteries no longer rule the world of thought and beauty; human life is the governing power, not that which lies beyond it. But the scientific workers are progressing, not so much by their own will as by sheer force of circumstances, towards the far line which divides things interpretable from things uninterpretable. Every fresh discovery drives them a step onward. Therefore do I very highly esteem the knowledge obtained by work and experiment.

But intuitive knowledge is an entirely different thing. It is not acquired in any way, but is, so to speak, a faculty of the soul; not the animal soul, that which becomes a ghost after death, when lust or liking or the memory of ill deeds holds it to the neighborhood of human beings, but the divine soul which animates all the external forms of the individualized being.

This is, of course, a faculty which indwells in that soul, which is inherent. The would-be disciple has to arouse himself to the conscious-

[50]

ness of it by a fierce and resolute and indomitable effort of will. I use the word indomitable for a special reason. Only he who is untameable, who cannot be dominated, who knows he has to play the lord over men, over facts, over all things save his own divinity, can arouse this faculty. "With faith all things are possible." The skeptical laugh at faith and pride themselves on its absence from their own minds. The truth is that faith is a great engine, an enormous power, which in fact can accomplish all things. For it is the covenant or engagement between man's divine part and his lesser self.

The use of this engine is quite necessary in order to obtain intuitive knowledge; for unless a man believes such knowledge exists within himself how can he claim and use it?

Without it he is more helpless than any driftwood or wreckage on the great tides of the ocean. They are cast hither and thither indeed; so may a man be by the chances of fortune. But such adventures are purely external and of very small account. A slave may be dragged through the streets in chains, and yet retain the quiet soul of a philosopher, as was well seen in the person of Epictetus. A man may have every worldly prize in his possession, and stand absolute master of his personal fate, to all appearance, and yet he knows no peace, no certainty, because he is shaken within himself by every tide of thought that he touches on. And these changing tides do not merely sweep the man bodily hither and thither like driftwood on the water; that would be nothing. They enter into the gateways of his soul, and wash over that soul and make it blind and blank and void of all permanent intelligence, so that passing impressions affect it.

To make my meaning plainer I will use an illustration. Take an author at his writing, a painter at his canvas, a composer listening to the melodies that dawn upon his glad imagination; let any one of these workers pass his daily hours by a wide window looking on a busy street. The power of the animating life blinds sight and hearing alike, and the great traffic of

[52]

the city goes by like nothing but a passing pageant. But a man whose mind is empty, whose day is objectless, sitting at that same window, notes the passers-by and remembers the faces that chance to please or interest him. So it is with the mind in its relation to eternal truth. If it no longer transmits its fluctuations, its partial knowledge, its unreliable information to the soul, then in the inner place of peace already found when the first rule has been learned — in that inner place there leaps into flame the light of actual knowledge. Then the ears begin to hear. Very dimly, very faintly at first. And, indeed, so faint and tender are these first indications of the commencement of true actual life, that they are sometimes pushed aside as mere fancies, mere imaginings.

But before these are capable of becoming more than mere imaginings, the abyss of nothingness has to be faced in another form. The utter silence which can only come by closing the ears to all transitory sounds comes as a more appalling horror than even the formless emptiness of space. Our only mental conception of blank space is, I think, when reduced to its barest element of thought, that of black darkness. This is a great physical terror to most persons, and when regarded as an eternal and unchangeable fact, must mean to the mind the idea of annihilation rather than anything else. But it is the obliteration of one sense only; and the sound of a voice may come and bring comfort even in the profoundest darkness. The disciple, having found his way into this blackness, which is the fearful abyss, must then so shut the gates of his soul that no comforter can enter there nor any enemy. And it is in making this second effort that the fact of pain and pleasure being but one sensation becomes recognizable by those who have before been unable to perceive it. For when the solitude of silence is reached the soul hungers so fiercely and passionately for some sensation on which to rest, that a painful one would be as keenly welcomed as a pleasant one. When this consciousness is reached the courageous man by seizing and retaining it, may destroy

[54]

the "sensitiveness" at once. When the ear no longer discriminates between that which is pleasant or that which is painful, it will no longer be affected by the voices of others. And then it is safe and possible to open the doors of the soul.

"Sight" is the first effort, and the easiest, because it is accomplished partly by an intellectual effort. The intellect can conquer the heart, as is well known in ordinary life. Therefore, this preliminary step still lies within the dominion of matter. But the second step allows of no such assistance, nor of any material aid whatever. Of course, I mean by material aid the action of the brain, or emotions, or human soul. In compelling the ears to listen only to the eternal silence, the being we call man becomes something which is no longer man. A very superficial survey of the thousand and one influences which are brought to bear on us by others will show that this must be so. A disciple will fulfil all the duties of his manhood; but he will fulfil them according to his own sense of right, and not according to that of any person or body of persons. This is a very evident result of following the creed of knowledge instead of any of the blind creeds.

To obtain the pure silence necessary for the disciple, the heart and emotions, the brain and its intellectualisms, have to be put aside. Both are but mechanisms, which will perish with the span of man's life. It is the essence beyond, that which is the motive power, and makes man live, that is now compelled to rouse itself and act. Now is the greatest hour of danger. In the first trial men go mad with fear; of this first trial Bulwer Lytton wrote. No novelist has followed to the second trial, though some of the poets have. Its subtlety and great danger lies in the fact that in the measure of a man's strength is the measure of his chance of passing beyond it or coping with it at all. If he has power enough to awaken that unaccustomed part of himself, the supreme essence, then has he power to lift the gates of gold, then is he the true alchemist, in possession of the elixir of life.

[56]

It is at this point of experience that the occultist becomes separated from all other men and enters on to a life which is his own; on to the path of individual accomplishment instead of mere obedience to the genii which rule our earth. This raising of himself into an individual power does in reality identify him with the nobler forces of life and make him one with them. For they stand beyond the powers of this earth and the laws of this universe. Here lies man's only hope of success in the great effort; to leap right away from his present standpoint to his next and at once become an intrinsic part of the divine power as he has been an intrinsic part of the intellectual power, of the great nature to which he belongs. He stands always in advance of himself, if such a contradiction can be understood. It is the men who adhere to this position, who believe in their innate power of progress, and that of the whole race, who are the elder brothers, the pioneers. Each man has to accomplish the great leap for himself and without aid; yet it is something of a staff to lean on to know that

others have gone on that road. It is possible
that they have been lost in the abyss; no
matter, they have had the courage to enter it.
Why I say that it is possible they have been
lost in the abyss is because of this fact, that one
who has passed through is unrecognizable until
the other and altogether new condition is attained by both. It is unnecessary to enter upon
the subject of what that condition is at present.

I only say this, that in the early state in
which man is entering upon the silence he loses
knowledge of his friends, of his lovers, of all
who have been near and dear to him; and also
loses sight of his teachers and of those who
have preceded him on his way. I explain this
because scarce one passes through without
bitter complaint. Could but the mind grasp
beforehand that the silence must be complete,
surely this complaint need not arise as a hin-
drance on the path. Your teacher, or your
predecessor may hold your hand in his, and
give you the utmost sympathy the human heart
is capable of. But when the silence and the
darkness comes, you lose all knowledge of him;

you are alone and he cannot help you, not because his power is gone, but because you have invoked your great enemy.

By your great enemy, I mean yourself. If you have the power to face your own soul in the darkness and silence, you will have conquered the physical or animal self which dwells in sensation only.

This statement, I feel, will appear involved; but in reality it is quite simple. Man, when he has reached his fruition, and civilization is at its height, stands between two fires. Could he but claim his great inheritance, the encumbrance of the mere animal life would fall away from him without difficulty. But he does not do this, and so the races of men flower and then droop and die and decay off the face of the earth, however splendid the bloom may have been. And it is left to the individual to make this great effort; to refuse to be terrified by his greater nature, to refuse to be drawn back by his lesser or more material self. Every individual who accomplishes this is a redeemer of the race. He may not blazon forth his deeds, he may dwell in secret and silence; but it is a fact that he forms a link between man and his divine part; between the known and the unknown; between the stir of the market place and the stillness of the snow-capped Himalayas. He has not to go about among men in order to form this link; in the astral he *is* that link, and this fact makes him a being of another order from the rest of mankind. Even so early on the road towards knowledge, when he has but taken the second step, he finds his footing more certain, and becomes conscious that he is a recognized part of a whole.

This is one of the contradictions in life which occur so constantly that they afford fuel to the fiction writer. The occultist finds them become much more marked as he endeavors to live the life he has chosen. As he retreats within himself and becomes self-dependent, he finds himself more definitely becoming part of a great tide of definite thought and feeling. When he has learned the first lesson, conquered the hunger of the heart, and refused to live on the love of others, he finds himself more capable of inspiring love. As he flings life away it comes to him in a new form and with a new meaning. The world has always been a place with many contradictions in it, to the man; when he becomes a disciple he finds life is describable as a series of paradoxes. This is a fact in nature, and the reason for it is intelligible enough. Man's soul "dwells like a star apart," even that of the vilest among us; while his consciousness is under the law of vibratory and sensuous life. This alone is enough to cause those complications of character which are the material for the novelist; every man is a mystery, to friend and enemy alike, and to himself. His motives are often undiscoverable, and he cannot probe to them or know why he does this or that. The disciple's effort is that of awakening consciousness in this starry part of himself, where his power and divinity lie sleeping. As this consciousness becomes awakened, the contradictions in the man himself become more marked than ever; and so do the paradoxes which he lives through. For, of course man creates his own life; and "adventures are to the adventurous" is one of those wise proverbs which are drawn from actual fact, and cover the whole area of human experience.

Pressure on the divine part of man re-acts upon the animal part. As the silent soul awakes it makes the ordinary life of the man more purposeful, more vital, more real, and responsible. To keep to the two instances already mentioned, the occultist who has withdrawn into his own citadel has found his strength; immediately he becomes aware of the demands of duty upon him. He does not obtain his strength by his own right, but because he is a part of the whole; and as soon as he is safe from the vibration of life and can stand unshaken, the outer world cries out to him to come and labour in it. So with the heart. When it no longer wishes to take, it is called upon to give abundantly.

"Light on the Path" has been called a book of paradoxes, and very justly; what else could it be, when it deals with the actual personal experience of the disciple?

[62]

To have acquired the astral senses of sight and hearing; or in other words to have attained perception and opened the doors of the soul, are gigantic tasks and may take the sacrifice of many successive incarnations. And yet, when the will has reached its strength, the whole miracle may be worked in a second of time. Then is the disciple the servant of Time no longer.

These two first steps are negative; that is to say they imply retreat from a present condition of things rather than advance towards another. The two next are active, implying the advance into another state of being.

△

III

"Before the voice can speak in the presence of the Masters."

Speech is the power of communication; the moment of entrance into active life is marked by its attainment.

And now, before I go any further, let me explain a little the way in which the rules written down in "Light on the Path" are arranged. The first seven of those which are numbered are sub-divisions of the two first unnumbered rules, those with which I have dealt in the two preceding papers. The numbered rules were simply an effort of mine to make the unnumbered ones more intelligible. "Eight" to "fifteen" of these numbered rules belong to this unnumbered rule which is now my text.

As I have said, these rules are written for all disciples, but for none else; they are not of interest to any other persons. Therefore I trust no one else will trouble to read these papers any further. The first two rules, which include the whole of that part of the effort which necessitates the use of the surgeon's knife, I will enlarge upon further if I am asked to do so. But the disciple is expected to deal with the snake, his lower self, unaided; to suppress his human passions and emotions by the force of his own will. He can only demand assistance of a master when this is accomplished, or at all events, partially so. Otherwise the gates and windows of his soul are blurred, and blinded, and darkened, and no knowledge can come to him. I am not, in these papers, purposing to tell a man how to deal with his own soul; I am simply giving, to the disciple, knowledge. That I am not writing, even now, so that all who run may read, is owing to the fact that super-nature prevents this by its own immutable laws.

The four rules which I have written down for those in the West who wish to study them, are as I have said, written in the ante-chamber of every living Brotherhood; I may add more, in the ante-chamber of every living or dead Brotherhood, or Order yet to be formed. When I speak of a Brotherhood or an Order, I do not mean an arbitrary constitution made by scholiasts and intellectualists; I mean an actual fact in super-nature, a stage of development towards the absolute God or Good. During this development the disciple encounters harmony, pure knowledge, pure truth, in different degrees, and, as he enters these degrees, he finds himself becoming part of what might be roughly described as a layer of human consciousness. He encounters his equals, men of his own self-less character, and with them his association becomes permanent and indissoluble, because founded on a vital likeness of nature. To them he becomes pledged by such vows as need no utterance or framework in ordinary words. This is one aspect of what I mean by a Brotherhood.

If the first rules are conquered, the disciple finds himself standing at the threshold. Then if his will is sufficiently resolute his power of

speech comes; a two-fold power. For, as he
advances now, he finds himself entering into
a state of blossoming, where every bud that
opens throws out its several rays or petals. If
he is to exercise his new gift, he must use it
in its two-fold character. He finds in himself
the power to speak in the presence of the
masters; in other words, he has the right to
demand contact with the divinest element of
that state of consciousness into which he has
entered. But he finds himself compelled, by
the nature of his position, to act in two ways
at the same time. He cannot send his voice up
to the heights where sit the gods till he has
penetrated to the deep places where their light
shines not at all. He has come within the grip
of an iron law. If he demands to become a
neophyte, he at once becomes a servant. Yet
his service is sublime, if only from the character of those who share it. For the masters
are also servants; they serve and claim their
reward afterwards. Part of their service is to
let their knowledge touch him; his first act of
service is to give some of that knowledge to

[67]

those who are not yet fit to stand where he stands. This is no arbitrary decision, made by any master or teacher or any such person, however divine. It is a law of that life which the disciple has entered upon.

Therefore was it written in the inner doorway of the lodges of the old Egyptian Brotherhood, "The laborer is worthy of his hire."

"Ask and ye shall have," sounds like something too easy and simple to be credible. But the disciple cannot "ask" in the mystic sense in which the word is used in this scripture until he has attained the power of helping others.

Why is this? Has the statement too dogmatic a sound?

Is it too dogmatic to say that a man must have foothold before he can spring? The position is the same. If help is given, if work is done, then there is an actual claim — not what we call a personal claim of payment, but the claim of co-nature. The divine give, they demand that you also shall give before you can be of their kin.

This law is discovered as soon as the disciple endeavors to speak. For speech is a gift which comes only to the disciple of power and knowledge. The spiritualist enters the psychic-astral world, but he does not find there any certain speech, unless he at once claims it and continues to do so. If he is interested in "phenomena," or the mere circumstance and accident of astral life, then he enters no direct ray of thought or purpose, he merely exists and amuses himself in the astral life as he has existed and amused himself in the physical life. Certainly there are one or two simple lessons which the psychic-astral can teach him, just as there are simple lessons which material and intellectual life teach him. And these lessons have to be learned; the man who proposes to enter upon the life of the disciple without having learned the early and simple lessons must always suffer from his ignorance. They are vital, and have to be studied in a vital manner; experienced through and through, over and over again, so that each part of the nature has been penetrated by them.

To return. In claiming the power of speech,

as it is called, the Neophyte cries out to the Great One who stands foremost in the ray of knowledge on which he has entered, to give him guidance. When he does this, his voice is hurled back by the power he has approached, and echoes down to the deep recesses of human ignorance. In some confused and blurred manner the news that there is knowledge and a beneficent power which teaches is carried to as many men as will listen to it. No disciple can cross the threshold without communicating this news, and placing it on record in some fashion or other.

He stands horror-struck at the imperfect and unprepared manner in which he has done this; and then comes the desire to do it well, and with the desire thus to help others comes the power. For it is a pure desire, this which comes upon him; he can gain no credit, no glory, no personal reward by fulfilling it. And therefore he obtains the power to fulfil it.

The history of the whole past, so far as we can trace it, shows very plainly that there is neither credit, glory, nor reward to be gained

by this first task which is given to the Neophyte. Mystics have always been sneered at,
and seers disbelieved; those who have had the
added power of intellect have left for posterity
their written record, which to most men appears unmeaning and visionary, even when the
authors have the advantage of speaking from a
far-off past. The disciple who undertakes the
task, secretly hoping for fame or success, to
appear as a teacher and apostle before the
world, fails even before his task is attempted,
and his hidden hypocrisy poisons his own soul,
and the souls of those he touches. He is
secretly worshiping himself, and this idolatrous
practice must bring its own reward.

The disciple who has the power of entrance,
and is strong enough to pass each barrier, will,
when the divine message comes to his spirit,
forget himself utterly in the new consciousness
which falls on him. If this lofty contact can
really rouse him, he becomes as one of the
divine in his desire to give rather than to take,
in his wish to help rather than be helped, in
his resolution to feed the hungry rather than

[71]

take manna from Heaven himself. His nature
is transformed, and the selfishness which
prompts men's actions in ordinary life suddenly
deserts him.

IV

"BEFORE THE VOICE CAN SPEAK IN THE PRESENCE OF THE MASTERS, IT MUST HAVE LOST THE POWER TO WOUND."

Those who give a merely passing and superficial attention to the subject of occultism — and their name is Legion — constantly inquire why, if adepts in life exist, they do not appear in the world and show their power. That the chief body of these wise ones should be understood to dwell beyond the fastnesses of the Himalayas, appears to be a sufficient proof that they are only figures of straw. Otherwise, why place them so far off?

Unfortunately, Nature has done this and not personal choice or arrangement. There are certain spots on the earth where the advance of "civilization" is unfelt, and the nineteenth century fever is kept at bay. In these favored places there is always time, always opportunity, for the realities of life; they are not crowded out by the doings of an inchoate, money-loving, pleasure seeking society. While there are adepts upon the earth, the earth must preserve to them places of seclusion. This is a fact in nature which is only an external expression of a profound fact in super-nature.

The demand of the neophyte remains unheard until the voice in which it is uttered has lost the power to wound. This is because the divine-astral life* is a place in which order reigns, just as it does in natural life. There is, of course, always the center and the circumference as there is in nature. Close to the central heart of life, on any plane, there is knowledge, there order reigns completely; and chaos makes dim and confused the outer margin of the circle. In fact, life in every form bears a more or less strong resemblance to a

*Of course every occultist knows by reading Eliphas Lévi and other authors that the "astral" plane is a plane of unequalized forces, and that a state of confusion necessarily prevails. But this does not apply to the "divine astral" plane, which is a plane where wisdom, and therefore order, prevails.

[74]

philosophic school. There are always the devo-
tees of knowledge who forget their own lives
in their pursuit of it; there are always the
flippant crowd who come and go — of such,
Epictetus said that it was as easy to teach
them philosophy as to eat custard with a fork.
The same state exists in the super-astral life;
and the adept has an even deeper and more
profound seclusion there in which to dwell.
This place of retreat is so safe, so sheltered,
that no sound which has discord in it can reach
his ears. Why should this be, will be asked at
once, if he is a being of such great powers as
those say who believe in his existence? The
answer seems very apparent. He serves humanity and identifies himself with the whole world;
he is ready to make vicarious sacrifice for it at
any moment — *by living not by dying for it.*
Why should he not die for it? Because he is
part of the great whole, and one of the most
valuable parts of it. Because he lives under
laws of order which he does not desire to
break. His life is not his own, but that of the
forces which work behind him. He is the

[75]

flower of humanity, the bloom which contains
the divine seed. He is, in his own person, a
treasure of the universal nature, which is
guarded and made safe in order that the fruition shall be perfected. It is only at definite
periods of the world's history that he is allowed
to go among the herd of men as their redeemer.
But for those who have the power to separate
themselves from this herd he is always at hand.
And for those who are strong enough to conquer the vices of the personal human nature, as
set forth in these four rules, he is consciously
at hand, easily recognized, ready to answer.

But this conquering of self implies a destruction of qualities which most men regard
as not only indestructible but desirable. The
"power to wound" includes much that men
value, not only in themselves, but in others
The instinct of self-defense and of self-preser-
vation is part of it; the idea that one has any
right or rights, either as citizen, or man, or
individual, the pleasant consciousness of self-
respect and of virtue. These are hard sayings
to many; yet they are true. For these words

that I am writing now, and those which I have written on this subject, are not in any sense my own. They are drawn from the traditions of the lodge of the Great Brotherhood, which was once the secret splendor of Egypt. The rules written in its ante-chamber were the same as those now written in the ante-chamber of existing schools. Through all time the wise men have lived apart from the mass. And even when some temporary purpose or object induces one of them to come into the midst of human life, his seclusion and safety is preserved as completely as ever. It is part of his inheritance, part of his position, he has an actual title to it, and can no more put it aside than the Duke of Westminster can say he does not choose to be the Duke of Westminster. In the various great cities of the world an adept lives for a while from time to time, or perhaps only passes through; but all are occasionally aided by the actual power and presence of one of these men. Here in London, as in Paris and St. Petersburgh, there are men high in development. But they are only known as mystics by those who have the power to recognize; the power given by the conquering of self. Otherwise how could they exist, even for an hour, in such a mental and psychic atmosphere as is created by the confusion and disorder of a city? Unless protected and made safe their own growth would be interfered with, their work injured. And the neophyte may meet an adept in the flesh, may live in the same house with him, and yet be unable to recognize him, and unable to make his own voice heard by him. For no nearness in space, no closeness of relations, no daily intimacy, can do away with the inexorable laws which give the adept his seclusion. No voice penetrates to his inner hearing till it has become a divine voice, a voice which gives no utterance to the cries of self. Any lesser appeal would be as useless, as much a waste of energy and power, as for mere children who are learning their alphabet to be taught it by a professor of philology. Until a man has become, in heart and spirit, a disciple, he has no existence for those who are teachers of disciples. And he becomes this by one method only

— the surrender of his personal humanity.

For the voice to have lost the power to wound, a man must have reached that point where he sees himself only as one of the vast multitudes that live; one of the sands washed hither and thither by the sea of vibratory existence. It is said that every grain of sand in the ocean bed does, in its turn, get washed up on to the shore and lie for a moment in the sunshine. So with human beings, they are driven hither and thither by a great force, and each, in his turn, finds the sunrays on him. When a man is able to regard his own life as part of a whole like this he will no longer struggle in order to obtain anything for himself. This is the surrender of personal rights. The ordinary man expects, not to take equal fortunes with the rest of the world, but in some points, about which he cares, to fare better than the others. The disciple does not expect this. Therefore, though he be, like Epictetus, a chained slave, he has no word to say about it. He knows that the wheel of life turns ceaselessly. Burne Jones has shown it in his marvellous picture — the wheel turns, and on it are bound the rich and the poor, the great and the small — each has his moment of good fortune when the wheel brings him uppermost — the King rises and falls, the poet is *feted* and forgotten, the slave is happy and afterwards discarded. Each in his turn is crushed as the wheel turns on. The disciple knows that this is so, and though it is his duty to make the utmost of the life that is his, he neither complains of it nor is elated by it, nor does he complain against the better fortune of others. All alike, as he well knows, are but learning a lesson; and he smiles at the socialist and the reformer who endeavor by sheer force to re-arrange circumstances which arise out of the forces of human nature itself. This is but kicking against the pricks; a waste of life and energy.

In realizing this a man surrenders his imagined individual rights, of whatever sort. That takes away one keen sting which is common to all ordinary men.

When the disciple has fully recognized that the very thought of individual rights is only

[80]

the outcome of the venomous quality in himself, that it is the hiss of the snake of self which poisons with its sting his own life and the lives of those about him, then he is ready to take part in a yearly ceremony which is open to all neophytes who are prepared for it. All weapons of defense and offense are given up; all weapons of mind and heart, and brain, and spirit. Never again can another man be regarded as a person who can be criticized or condemned; never again can the neophyte raise his voice in self-defense or excuse. From that ceremony he returns into the world as helpless, as unprotected, as a new-born child. That, indeed, is what he is. He has begun to be born again on to the higher plane of life, that breezy and well-lit plateau from whence the eyes see intelligently and regard the world with a new insight.

I have said, a little way back, that after parting with the sense of individual rights, the disciple must part also with the sense of self-respect and of virtue. This may sound a terrible doctrine, yet all occultists know well that it is not a doctrine, but a fact. He who thinks himself holier than another, he who has any pride in his own exemption from vice or folly, he who believes himself wise, or in any way superior to his fellow men, is incapable of discipleship. A man must become as a little child before he can enter into the kingdom of heaven.

Virtue and wisdom are sublime things; but if they create pride and a consciousness of separateness from the rest of humanity in the mind of a man, then they are only the snakes of self re-appearing in a finer form. At any moment he may put on his grosser shape and sting as fiercely as when he inspired the actions of a murderer who kills for gain or hatred, or a politician who sacrifices the mass for his own or his party's interests.

In fact, to have lost the power to wound, implies that the snake is not only scotched, but killed. When it is merely stupefied or lulled to sleep it awakes again and the disciple uses his knowledge and his power for his own ends, and is a pupil of the many masters of the black art, for the road to destruction is very broad and easy, and the way can be found blindfold. That it is the way to destruction is evident, for when a man begins to live for self he narrows his horizon steadily till at last the fierce driving inwards leaves him but the space of a pin's-head to dwell in. We have all seen this phenomenon occur in ordinary life. A man who becomes selfish isolates himself, grows less interesting and less agreeable to others. The sight is an awful one, and people shrink from a very selfish person at last, as from a beast of prey. How much more awful is it when it occurs on the more advanced plane of life, with the added powers of knowledge, and through the greater sweep of successive incarnations!

Therefore I say, pause and think well upon the threshold. For if the demand of the neophyte is made without the complete purification, it will not penetrate the seclusion of the divine adept, but will evoke the terrible forces which attend upon the black side of our human nature.

V

"BEFORE THE SOUL CAN STAND IN THE
PRESENCE OF THE MASTERS, ITS FEET MUST
BE WASHED IN THE BLOOD OF THE HEART."

The word soul, as used here, means the
divine soul, or "starry spirit."

"To be able to stand is to have confidence";
and to have confidence means that the disciple
is sure of himself, that he has surrendered his
emotions, his very self, even his humanity;
that he is incapable of fear and unconscious of
pain; that his whole consciousness is centered
in the divine life, which is expressed symboli-
cally by the term "the Masters"; that he has
neither eyes, nor ears, nor speech, nor power,
save in and for the divine ray on which his
highest sense has touched. Then is he fearless,
free from suffering, free from anxiety or dismay; his soul stands without shrinking or
desire of postponement, in the full blaze of the

divine light which penetrates through and through his being. Then he has come into his inheritance and can claim his kinship with the teachers of men; he is upright, he has raised his head, he breathes the same air that they do.

But before it is in any way possible for him to do this, the feet of the soul must be washed in the blood of the heart.

The sacrifice, or surrender of the heart of man, and its emotions, is the first of the rules; it involves the "attaining of an equilibrium which cannot be shaken by personal emotion." This is done by the stoic philosopher; he, too, stands aside and looks equably upon his own sufferings, as well as on those of others.

In the same way that "tears" in the language of occultists expresses the soul of emotion, not its material appearance, so blood expresses, not that blood which is an essential of physical life, but the vital creative principle in man's nature, which drives him into human life in order to experience pain and pleasure, joy and sorrow. When he has let the blood flow from the heart he stands before the Mas-

[85]

ters as a pure spirit which no longer wishes to incarnate for the sake of emotion and experience. Through great cycles of time successive incarnations in gross matter may yet be his lot; but he no longer desires them, the crude wish to live has departed from him. When he takes upon him man's form in the flesh he does it in the pursuit of a divine object, to accomplish the work of "the Masters," and for no other end. He looks neither for pleasure nor pain, asks for no heaven, and fears no hell; yet he has entered upon a great inheritance which is not so much a compensation for these things surrendered, as a state which simply blots out the memory of them. He lives now not in the world, but with it; his horizon has extended itself to the width of the whole universe.

△

KARMA

CONSIDER with me that the individual existence is a rope which stretches from the
infinite to the infinite and has no end and no
commencement, neither is it capable of being
broken. This rope is formed of innumerable
fine threads, which, lying closely together,
form its thickness. These threads are colorless,
are perfect in their qualities of straightness,
strength, and levelness. This rope, passing as
it does through all places, suffers strange
accidents. Very often a thread is caught and
becomes attached, or perhaps is only violently
pulled away from its even way. Then for a
great time it is disordered, and it disorders the
whole. Sometimes one is stained with dirt or
with color, and not only does the stain run on
further than the spot of contact, but it discolors
other of the threads. And remember that the
threads are living — are like electric wires,
more, are like quivering nerves. How far, then,

must the stain, the drag awry, be communicated! But eventually the long strands, the living threads which in their unbroken continuity form the individual, pass out of the shadow into the shine. Then the threads are no longer colorless, but golden; once more they lie together, level. Once more harmony is established between them; and from that harmony within the greater harmony is perceived.

This illustration presents but a small portion — a single side of the truth: it is less than a fragment. Yet, dwell on it; by its aid you may be led to perceive more. What it is necessary first to understand is, not that the future is arbitrarily formed by any separate acts of the present, but that the whole of the future is in unbroken continuity with the present as the present is with the past. On one plane, from one point of view, the illustration of the rope is correct.

It is said that a little attention to occultism produces great Karmic results. That is because it is impossible to give any attention to occultism without making a definite choice between what are familiarly called good and evil. The first step in occultism brings the student to the tree of knowledge. He must pluck and eat; he must choose. No longer is he capable of the indecision of ignorance. He goes on, either on the good or on the evil path. And to step definitely and knowingly even but one step on either path produces great Karmic results. The mass of men walk waveringly, uncertain as to the goal they aim at; their standard of life is indefinite; consequently their Karma operates in a confused manner. But when once the threshold of knowledge is reached, the confusion begins to lessen, and consequently the Karmic results increase enormously, because all are acting in the same direction on all the different planes: for the occultist cannot be half-hearted, nor can he return when he has passed the threshold. These things are as impossible as that the man should become the child again. The individuality has approached the state of responsibility by reason of growth; it cannot recede from it.

He who would escape from the bondage of

Karma must raise his individuality out of the shadow into the shine; must so elevate his existence that these threads do not come in contact with soiling substances, do not become so attached as to be pulled awry. He simply lifts himself out of the region in which Karma operates. He does not leave the existence which he is experiencing because of that. The ground may be rough and dirty, or full of rich flowers whose pollen stains, and of sweet substances that cling and become attachments — but overhead there is always the free sky. He who desires to be Karmaless must look to the air for a home; and after that to the ether. He who desires to form good Karma will meet with many confusions, and in the effort to sow rich seed for his own harvesting may plant a thousand weeds, and among them the giant. Desire to sow no seed for your own harvesting; desire only to sow that seed the fruit of which shall feed the world. You are a part of the world; in giving it food you feed yourself. Yet in even this thought there lurks a great danger which starts forward and faces the disciple, who has for long thought himself working for good, while in his inmost soul he has perceived only evil; that is, he has thought himself to be intending great benefit to the world while all the time he has unconsciously embraced the thought of Karma, and the great benefit he works for is for himself. A man may refuse to allow himself to think of reward. But in that very refusal is seen the fact that reward is desired. And it is useless for the disciple to strive to learn by means of checking himself. The soul must be unfettered, the desires free. But until they are fixed only on that state wherein there is neither reward nor punishment, good nor evil, it is in vain that he endeavors. He may seem to make great progress, but some day he will come face to face with his own soul, and will recognize that when he came to the tree of knowledge he chose the bitter fruit and not the sweet; and then the veil will fall utterly, and he will give up his freedom and become a slave of desire. Therefore be warned, you who are but turning toward the life of occultism. Learn now that there is no cure for

desire, no cure for the love of reward, no cure
for the misery of longing, save in the fixing
of the sight and hearing upon that which is
invisible and soundless. Begin even now to
practice it, and so a thousand serpents will be
kept from your path. Live in the eternal.

The operations of the actual laws of Karma
are not to be studied until the disciple has
reached the point at which they no longer affect
himself. The initiate has a right to demand
the secrets of nature and to know the rules
which govern human life. He obtains this right
by having escaped from the limits of nature
and by having freed himself from the rules
which govern human life. He has become a
recognized portion of the divine element, and
is no longer affected by that which is temporary. He then obtains a knowledge of the laws
which govern temporary conditions. Therefore
you who desire to understand the laws of
Karma, attempt first to free yourself from
these laws; and this can only be done by
fixing your attention on that which is unaffected
by those laws.

THROUGH THE GATES OF GOLD

Through the
Gates of Gold

A FRAGMENT OF THOUGHT

Theosophical University Press
Pasadena, California

Once, as I sat alone writing, a mysterious Visitor entered my study, unannounced, and stood beside me. I forgot to ask who he was or why he entered so unceremoniously, for he began to tell me of the Gates of Gold. He spoke from knowledge, and from the fire of his speech I caught faith. I have written down his words; but, alas, I cannot hope that the fire shall burn so brightly in my writing as in his speech.

M. C.

PROLOGUE

EVERY man has a philosophy of life of his own, except the true philosopher. The most ignorant boor has some conception of his object in living, and definite ideas as to the easiest and wisest way of attaining that object. The man of the world is often, unconsciously to himself, a philosopher of the first rank. He deals with his life on principles of the clearest character, and refuses to let his position be shattered by chance disaster. The man of thought and imagination has less certainty, and finds himself continually unable to formulate his ideas on that subject most profoundly interesting to human nature, — human life itself. The true philosopher is the one who would lay no claim to the name whatever, who has discovered that the mystery of life is unapproachable by ordinary thought, just as the true scientist confesses his complete ignorance of the principles which lie behind science.

[1]

Whether there is any mode of thought or any effort of the mind which will enable a man to grasp the great principles that evidently exist as causes in human life, is a question no ordinary thinker can determine. Yet the dim consciousness that there is cause behind the effects we see, that there is order ruling the chaos and sublime harmony pervading the discords, haunts the eager souls of the earth, and makes them long for vision of the unseen and knowledge of the unknowable.

Why long and look for that which is beyond all hope until the inner eyes are opened? Why not piece together the fragments that we have at hand, and see whether from them some shape cannot be given to the vast puzzle?

CHAPTER I

I

WE are all acquainted with that stern thing called misery, which pursues man, and strangely enough, as it seems at first, pursues him with no vague or uncertain method, but with a positive and unbroken pertinacity. Its presence is not absolutely continuous, else man must cease to live; but its pertinacity is without any break. There is always the shadowy form of despair standing behind man ready to touch him with its terrible finger if for too long he finds himself content. What has given this ghastly shape the right to haunt us from the hour we are born until the hour we die? What has given it the right to stand always at our door, keeping that door ajar with its impalpable yet plainly horrible hand, ready to enter at the moment it sees fit? The greatest philosopher that ever lived succumbs before it at last; and he only is a philosopher, in any sane sense, who

[3]

recognizes the fact that it is irresistible, and knows that like all other men he must suffer soon or late. It is part of the heritage of men, this pain and distress; and he who determines that nothing shall make him suffer, does but cloak himself in a profound and chilly selfishness. This cloak may protect him from pain; it will also separate him from pleasure. If peace is to be found on earth, or any joy in life, it cannot be by closing up the gates of feeling, which admit us to the loftiest and most vivid part of our existence. Sensation, as we obtain it through the physical body, affords us all that induces us to live in that shape. It is inconceivable that any man would care to take the trouble of breathing, unless the act brought with it a sense of satisfaction. So it is with every deed of every instant of our life. We live because it is pleasant even to have the sensation of pain. It is sensation we desire, else we would with one accord taste of the deep waters of oblivion, and the human race would become extinct. If this is the case in the physical life, it is evidently the case with the

[4]

life of the emotions, — the imagination, the sensibilities, all those fine and delicate formations which, with the marvellous recording mechanism of the brain, make up the inner or subtile man. Sensation is that which makes their pleasure; an infinite series of sensations is life to them. Destroy the sensation which makes them wish to persevere in the experiment of living, and there is nothing left. Therefore the man who attempts to obliterate the sense of pain, and who proposes to maintain an equal state whether he is pleased or hurt, strikes at the very root of life, and destroys the object of his own existence. And that must apply, so far as our present reasoning or intuitive powers can show us, to every state, even to that of the Oriental's longed-for Nirvana. This condition can only be one of infinitely subtiler and more exquisite sensation, if it is a state at all, and not annihilation; and according to the experience of life from which we are at present able to judge, increased subtility of sensation means increased vividness, — as, for instance, a man of sensibility

[5]

and imagination feels more in consequence of
the unfaithfulness or faithfulness of a friend
than can a man of even the grossest physical
nature feel through the medium of the senses.
Thus it is clear that the philosopher who
refuses to feel, leaves himself no place to
retreat to, not even the distant and unattainable Nirvanic goal. He can only deny himself
his heritage of life, which is in other words
the right of sensation. If he chooses to sacrifice that which makes him man, he must be
content with mere idleness of consciousness, —
a condition compared to which the oyster's
is a life of excitement.

But no man is able to accomplish such a
feat. The fact of his continued existence proves
plainly that he still desires sensation, and
desires it in such positive and active form that
the desire must be gratified in physical life. It
would seem more practical not to deceive one's
self by the sham of stoicism, not to attempt
renunciation of that with which nothing would
induce one to part. Would it not be a bolder
policy, a more promising mode of solving the

great enigma of existence, to grasp it, to take hold firmly and to demand of it the mystery of itself? If men will but pause and consider what lessons they have learned from pleasure and pain, much might be guessed of that strange thing which causes these effects. But men are prone to turn away hastily from self-study, or from any close analysis of human nature. Yet there must be a science of life as intelligible as any of the methods of the schools. The science is unknown, it is true, and its existence is merely guessed, merely hinted at, by one or two of our more advanced thinkers. The development of a science is only the discovery of what is already in existence; and chemistry is as magical and incredible now to the ploughboy as the science of life is to the man of ordinary perceptions. Yet there may be, and there must be, a seer who perceives the growth of the new knowledge as the earliest dabblers in the experiments of the laboratory saw the system of knowledge now attained evolving itself out of nature for man's use and benefit.

[7]

II

Doubtless many more would experiment in suicide, as many now do, in order to escape from the burden of life, if they could be convinced that in that manner oblivion might be found. But he who hesitates before drinking the poison from the fear of only inviting change of mode of existence, and perhaps a more active form of misery, is a man of more knowledge than the rash souls who fling themselves wildly on the unknown, trusting to its kindliness. The waters of oblivion are something very different from the waters of death, and the human race cannot become extinct by means of death while the law of birth still operates. Man returns to physical life as the drunkard returns to the flagon of wine, — he knows not why, except that he desires the sensation produced by life as the drunkard desires the sensation produced by wine. The true waters of oblivion lie far behind our consciousness, and can only be reached by ceasing to exist in that consciousness, — by ceasing to exert the will which makes us full of senses and sensibilities.

Why does not the creature man return into that great womb of silence whence he came, and remain in peace, as the unborn child is at peace before the impetus of life has reached it? He does not do so because he hungers for pleasure and pain, joy and grief, anger and love. The unfortunate man will maintain that he has no desire for life; and yet he proves his words false by living. None can compel him to live; the galley-slave may be chained to his oar, but his life cannot be chained to his body. The superb mechanism of the human body is as useless as an engine whose fires are not lit, if the will to live ceases, — that will which we maintain resolutely and without pause, and which enables us to perform the tasks which otherwise would fill us with dismay, as, for instance, the momently drawing in and giving out of the breath. Such herculean efforts as this we carry on without complaint, and indeed with pleasure, in order that we may exist in the midst of innumerable sensations.

[9]

And more; we are content, for the most part, to go on without object or aim, without any idea of a goal or understanding of which way we are going. When the man first becomes aware of this aimlessness, and is dimly conscious that he is working with great and constant efforts, and without any idea towards what end those efforts are directed, then descends on him the misery of nineteenth-century thought. He is lost and bewildered, and without hope. He becomes sceptical, disillusioned, weary, and asks the apparently unanswerable question whether it is indeed worth while to draw his breath for such unknown and seemingly unknowable results. But are these results unknowable? At least, to ask a lesser question, is it impossible to make a guess as to the direction in which our goal lies?

III

This question, born of sadness and weariness, which seems to us essentially part of the spirit of the nineteenth century, is in fact a question which must have been asked all through the ages. Could we go back throughout history intelligently, no doubt we should find that it came always with the hour when the flower of civilization had blown to its full, and when its petals were but slackly held together. The natural part of man has reached then its utmost height; he has rolled the stone up the Hill of Difficulty only to watch it roll back again when the summit is reached, — as in Egypt, in Rome, in Greece. Why this useless labor? Is it not enough to produce a weariness and sickness unutterable, to be forever accomplishing a task only to see it undone again? Yet that is what man has done throughout history, so far as our limited knowledge reaches. There is one summit to which, by immense and united efforts, he attains, where there is a great and brilliant efflorescence of all the intellectual, mental, and material part of his nature. The climax of sensuous perfection is reached, and then his hold weakens, his power grows less, and he falls back, through despondency and satiety, to barbarism. Why does he not stay on this hill-top he has reached, and look away to the mountains beyond, and resolve to scale those greater heights? Because he is ignorant, and seeing a great glittering in the distance, drops his eyes bewildered and dazzled, and goes back for rest to the shadowy side of his familiar hill. Yet there is now and then one brave enough to gaze fixedly on this glittering, and to decipher something of the shape within it. Poets and philosophers, thinkers and teachers, — all those who are the "elder brothers of the race," — have beheld this sight from time to time, and some among them have recognized in the bewildering glitter the outlines of the Gates of Gold.

Those Gates admit us to the sanctuary of man's own nature, to the place whence his life-power comes, and where he is priest of the shrine of life. That it is possible to enter here, to pass through those Gates, some one or two have shown us. Plato, Shakespeare, and a few other strong ones have gone through and spoken to us in veiled language on the near

[12]

side of the Gates. When the strong man has crossed the threshold he speaks no more to those at the other side. And even the words he utters when he is outside are so full of mystery, so veiled and profound, that only those who follow in his steps can see the light within them.

IV

What men desire is to ascertain how to exchange pain for pleasure; that is, to find out in what way consciousness may be regulated in order that the sensation which is most agreeable is the one that is experienced. Whether this can be discovered by dint of human thought is at least a question worth considering.

If the mind of man is turned upon any given subject with a sufficient concentration, he obtains illumination with regard to it sooner or later. The particular individual in whom the final illumination appears is called a genius,

[13]

an inventor, one inspired; but he is only the crown of a great mental work created by unknown men about him, and receding back from him through long vistas of distance. Without them he would not have had his material to deal with. Even the poet requires innumerable poetasters to feed upon. He is the essence of the poetic power of his time, and of the times before him. It is impossible to separate an individual of any species from his kin.

If, therefore, instead of accepting the unknown as unknowable, men were *with one accord* to turn their thoughts towards it, those Golden Gates would not remain so inexorably shut. It does but need a strong hand to push them open. The courage to enter them is the courage to search the recesses of one's own nature without fear and without shame. In the fine part, the essence, the flavor of the man, is found the key which unlocks those great Gates. And when they open, what is it that is found?

Voices here and there in the long silence

of the ages speak to answer that question. Those who have passed through have left words behind them as legacies to others of their kin. In these words we can find definite indications of what is to be looked for beyond the Gates. But only those who desire to go that way read the meaning hidden within the words. Scholars, or rather scholiasts, read the sacred books of different nations, the poetry and the philosophy left by enlightened minds, and find in it all the merest materiality. Imagination glorifying legends of nature, or exaggerating the psychic possibilities of man, explains to them all that they find in the Bibles of humanity.

What is to be found within the words of those books is to be found in each one of us; and it is impossible to find in literature or through any channel of thought that which does not exist in the man who studies. This is of course an evident fact known to all real students. But it has to be especially remembered in reference to this profound and obscure subject, as men so readily believe that nothing

[15]

can exist for others where they themselves find emptiness.

One thing is soon perceived by the man who reads: those who have gone before have not found that the Gates of Gold lead to oblivion. On the contrary, sensation becomes real for the first time when that threshold is crossed. But it is of a new order, an order unknown to us now, and by us impossible to appreciate without at least some clew as to its character. This clew can be obtained undoubtedly by any student who cares to go through all the literature accessible to us. That mystic books and manuscripts exist, but remain inaccessible simply because there is no man ready to read the first page of any one of them, becomes the conviction of all who have studied the subject sufficiently. For there must be the continuous line all through: we see it go from dense ignorance up to intelligence and wisdom; it is only natural that it should go on to intuitive knowledge and to inspiration. Some scant fragments we have of these great gifts of man; where, then, is the whole of which they must be a part? Hidden behind the thin yet seemingly impassable veil which hides it from us as it hid all science, all art, all powers of man till he had the courage to tear away the screen. That courage comes only of conviction. When once man believes that the thing exists which he desires, he will obtain it at any cost. The difficulty in this case lies in man's incredulity. It requires a great tide of thought and attention to set in towards the unknown region of man's nature in order that its gates may be unlocked and its glorious vistas explored.

That it is worth while to do this whatever the hazard may be, all must allow who have asked the sad question of the nineteenth century, — Is life worth living? Surely it is sufficient to spur man to new effort, — the suspicion that beyond civilization, beyond mental culture, beyond art and mechanical perfection, there is a new, another gateway, admitting to the realities of life.

V

When it seems as if the end was reached, the goal attained, and that man has no more to do, — just then, when he appears to have no choice but between eating and drinking and living in his comfort as the beasts do in theirs, and scepticism which is death, — then it is that in fact, if he will but look, the Golden Gates are before him. With the culture of the age within him and assimilated perfectly, so that he is himself an incarnation of it, then he is fit to attempt the great step which is absolutely possible, yet is attempted by so few even of those who are fitted for it. It is so seldom attempted, partly because of the profound difficulties which surround it, but much more because man does not realize that this is actually the direction in which pleasure and satisfaction are to be obtained.

There are certain pleasures which appeal to each individual; every man knows that in one layer or another of sensation he finds his chief delight. Naturally he turns to this systematically through life, just as the sunflower

[18]

turns to the sun and the water-lily leans on the water. But he struggles throughout with an awful fact which oppresses him to the soul, — that no sooner has he obtained his pleasure than he loses it again and has once more to go in search of it. More than that; he never actually reaches it, for it eludes him at the final moment. This is because he endeavors to seize that which is untouchable and satisfy his soul's hunger for sensation by contact with external objects. How can that which is external satisfy or even please the inner man, — the thing which reigns within and has no eyes for matter, no hands for touch of objects, no senses with which to apprehend that which is outside its magic walls? Those charmed barriers which surround it are limitless, for it is everywhere; it is to be discovered in all living things, and no part of the universe can be conceived of without it, if that universe is regarded as a coherent whole. And unless that point is granted at the outset it is useless to consider the subject of life at all. Life is indeed meaningless unless it is universal and coher-

[19]

ent, and unless we maintain our existence by reason of the fact that we are part of that which is, not by reason of our own being.

This is one of the most important factors in the development of man, the recognition — profound and complete recognition — of the law of universal unity and coherence. The separation which exists between individuals, between worlds, between the different poles of the universe and of life, the mental and physical fantasy called space, is a nightmare of the human imagination. That nightmares exist, and exist only to torment, every child knows; and what we need is the power of discrimination between the phantasmagoria of the brain, which concern ourselves only, and the phantasmagoria of daily life, in which others also are concerned. This rule applies also to the larger case. It concerns no one but ourselves that we live in a nightmare of unreal horror, and fancy ourselves alone in the universe and capable of independent action, so long as our associates are those only who are a part of the dream; but when

we desire to speak with those who have tried
the Golden Gates and pushed them open, then
it is very necessary — in fact it is essential —
to discriminate, and not bring into our life the
confusions of our sleep. If we do, we are
reckoned as madmen, and fall back into the
darkness where there is no friend but chaos.
This chaos has followed every effort of man
that is written in history; after civilization has
flowered, the flower falls and dies, and winter
and darkness destroy it. While man refuses
to make the effort of discrimination which
would enable him to distinguish between the
shapes of night and the active figures of day,
this must inevitably happen.

But if man has the courage to resist this
reactionary tendency, to stand steadily on the
height he has reached and put out his foot in
search of yet another step, why should he
not find it? There is nothing to make one
suppose the pathway to end at a certain point,
except that tradition which has declared it is
so, and which men have accepted and hug to
themselves as a justification for their indolence.

[21]

VI

Indolence is, in fact, the curse of man. As the Irish peasant and the cosmopolitan gypsy dwell in dirt and poverty out of sheer idleness, so does the man of the world live contented in sensuous pleasures for the same reason. The drinking of fine wines, the tasting of delicate food, the love of bright sights and sounds, of beautiful women and admirable surroundings, — these are no better for the cultivated man, no more satisfactory as a final goal of enjoyment for him, than the coarse amusements and gratifications of the boor are for the man without cultivation. There can be no final point, for life in every form is one vast series of fine gradations; and the man who elects to stand still at the point of culture he has reached, and to avow that he can go no further, is simply making an arbitrary statement for the excuse of his indolence. Of course there is a possibility of declaring that the gypsy is content in his dirt and poverty, and, because he is so, is as great a man as the most highly cultured. But he only is so while he is ignorant; the moment light enters the dim mind the whole man turns towards it. So it is on the higher platform; only the difficulty of penetrating the mind, of admitting the light, is even greater. The Irish peasant loves his whiskey, and while he can have it cares nothing for the great laws of morality and religion which are supposed to govern humanity and induce men to live temperately. The cultivated gourmand cares only for subtle tastes and perfect flavors; but he is as blind as the merest peasant to the fact that there is anything beyond such gratifications. Like the boor he is deluded by a mirage that oppresses his soul; and he fancies, having once obtained a sensuous joy that pleases him, to give himself the utmost satisfaction by endless repetition, till at last he reaches madness. The bouquet of the wine he loves enters his soul and poisons it, leaving him with no thoughts but those of sensuous desire; and he is in the same hopeless state as the man who dies mad with drink. What good has the drunkard obtained by his madness? None; pain has at last swallowed up pleasure utterly, and death steps in to terminate the agony. The man suffers the final penalty for his persistent ignorance of a law of nature as inexorable as that of gravitation, — a law which forbids a man to stand still. Not twice can the same cup of pleasure be tasted; the second time it must contain either a grain of poison or a drop of the elixir of life.

The same argument holds good with regard to intellectual pleasures; the same law operates. We see men who are the flower of their age in intellect, who pass beyond their fellows and tower over them, entering at last upon a fatal treadmill of thought, where they yield to the innate indolence of the soul and begin to delude themselves by the solace of repetition. Then comes the barrenness and lack of vitality, — that unhappy and disappointing state into which great men too often enter when middle life is just passed. The fire of youth, the vigor of the young intellect, conquers the inner inertia and makes the man scale heights of thought and fill his mental

[24]

lungs with the free air of the mountains. But then at last the physical reaction sets in; the physical machinery of the brain loses its powerful impetus and begins to relax its efforts, simply because the youth of the body is at an end. Now the man is assailed by the great tempter of the race who stands forever on the ladder of life waiting for those who climb so far. He drops the poisoned drop into the ear, and from that moment all consciousness takes on a dulness, and the man becomes terrified lest life is losing its possibilities for him. He rushes back on to a familiar platform of experience, and there finds comfort in touching a well-known chord of passion or emotion. And too many having done this linger on, afraid to attempt the unknown, and satisfied to touch continually that chord which responds most readily. By this means they get the assurance that life is still burning within them. But at last their fate is the same as that of the gourmand and the drunkard. The power of the spell lessens daily as the machinery which feels loses its vitality; and the man endeavors to revive the old excitement and fervor by striking the note more violently, by hugging the thing that makes him feel, by drinking the cup of poison to its fatal dregs. And then he is lost; madness falls on his soul, as it falls on the body of the drunkard. Life has no longer any meaning for him, and he rushes wildly into the abysses of intellectual insanity. A lesser man who commits this great folly wearies the spirits of others by a dull clinging to familiar thought, by a persistent hugging of the treadmill which he asserts to be the final goal. The cloud that surrounds him is as fatal as death itself, and men who once sat at his feet turn away grieved, and have to look back at his early words in order to remember his greatness.

VII

What is the cure for this misery and waste of effort? Is there one? Surely life itself has a logic in it and a law which makes existence possible; otherwise chaos and madness would be the only state which would be attainable.

When a man drinks his first cup of pleasure his soul is filled with the unutterable joy that comes with a first, a fresh sensation. The drop of poison that he puts into the second cup, and which, if he persists in that folly, has to become doubled and trebled till at last the whole cup is poison, — that is the ignorant desire for repetition and intensification; this evidently means death, according to all analogy. The child becomes the man; he cannot retain his childhood and repeat and intensify the pleasures of childhood except by paying the inevitable price and becoming an idiot. The plant strikes its roots into the ground and throws up green leaves; then it blossoms and bears fruit. That plant which will only make roots or leaves, pausing persistently in its development, is regarded by the gardener as a thing which is useless and must be cast out.

The man who chooses the way of effort, and refuses to allow the sleep of indolence to dull his soul, finds in his pleasures a new and finer joy each time he tastes them, — a something subtile and remote which removes them

[27]

more and more from the state in which mere sensuousness is all; this subtile essence is that elixir of life which makes man immortal. He who tastes it and who will not drink unless it is in the cup finds life enlarge and the world grow great before his eager eyes. He recognizes the soul within the woman he loves, and passion becomes peace; he sees within his thought the finer qualities of spiritual truth, which is beyond the action of our mental machinery, and then instead of entering on the treadmill of intellectualisms he rests on the broad back of the eagle of intuition and soars into the fine air where the great poets found their insight; he sees within his own power of sensation, of pleasure in fresh air and sunshine, in food and wine, in motion and rest, the possibilities of the subtile man, the thing which dies not either with the body or the brain. The pleasures of art, of music, of light and loveliness, — within these forms, which men repeat till they find only the forms, he sees the glory of the Gates of Gold, and passes through to find the new life beyond which intoxicates and

[28]

strengthens, as the keen mountain air intoxicates and strengthens, by its very vigor. But if he has been pouring, drop by drop, more and more of the elixir of life into his cup, he is strong enough to breathe this intense air and to live upon it. Then if he die or if he live in physical form, alike he goes on and finds new and finer joys, more perfect and satisfying experiences, with every breath he draws in and gives out.

CHAPTER II

I

THERE is no doubt that at the entrance on a new phase of life something has to be given up. The child, when it has become the man, puts away childish things. Saint Paul showed in these words, and in many others which he has left us, that he had tasted of the elixir of life, that he was on his way towards the Gates of Gold. With each drop of the divine draught which is put into the cup of pleasure something is purged away from that cup to make room for the magic drop. For Nature deals with her children generously: man's cup is always full to the brim; and if he chooses to taste of the fine and life-giving essence, he must cast away something of the grosser and less sensitive part of himself. This has to be done daily, hourly, momently, in order that the draught of life may steadily increase. And to do this unflinchingly, a man must be his own

[30]

schoolmaster, must recognize that he is always in need of wisdom, must be ready to practise any austerities, to use the birch-rod unhesitatingly against himself, in order to gain his end. It becomes evident to any one who regards the subject seriously, that only a man who has the potentialities in him both of the voluptuary and the stoic has any chance of entering the Golden Gates. He must be capable of testing and valuing to its most delicate fraction every joy existence has to give; and he must be capable of denying himself all pleasure, and that without suffering from the denial. When he has accomplished the development of this double possibility, then he is able to begin sifting his pleasures and taking away from his consciousness those which belong absolutely to the man of clay. When those are put back, there is the next range of more refined pleasures to be dealt with. The dealing with these which will enable a man to find the essence of life is not the method pursued by the stoic philosopher. The stoic does not allow that there is joy within pleasure, and by denying himself the one loses the other. But the true philosopher, who has studied life itself without being bound by any system of thought, sees that the kernel is within the shell, and that, instead of crunching up the whole nut like a gross and indifferent feeder, the essence of the thing is obtained by cracking the shell and casting it away. All emotion, all sensation, lends itself to this process, else it could not be a part of man's development, an essential of his nature. For that there is before him power, life, perfection, and that every portion of his passage thitherwards is crowded with the means of helping him to his goal, can only be denied by those who refuse to acknowledge life as apart from matter. Their mental position is so absolutely arbitrary that it is useless to encounter or combat it. Through all time the unseen has been pressing on the seen, the immaterial overpowering the material; through all time the signs and tokens of that which is beyond matter have been waiting for the men of matter to test and weigh them. Those who will not do so have chosen the place of pause

[32]

arbitrarily, and there is nothing to be done but let them remain there undisturbed, working that treadmill which they believe to be the utmost activity of existence.

II

There is no doubt that a man must educate himself to perceive that which is beyond matter, just as he must educate himself to perceive that which is in matter. Every one knows that the early life of a child is one long process of adjustment, of learning to understand the use of the senses with regard to their special provinces, and of practice in the exercise of difficult, complex, yet imperfect organs entirely in reference to the perception of the world of matter. The child is in earnest and works on without hesitation if he means to live. Some infants born into the light of earth shrink from it, and refuse to attack the immense task which is before them, and which must be accomplished in order to make life in matter possible.

These go back to the ranks of the unborn; we see them lay down their manifold instrument, the body, and fade into sleep. So it is with the great crowd of humanity when it has triumphed and conquered and enjoyed in the world of matter. The individuals in that crowd, which seems so powerful and confident in its familiar demesne, are infants in the presence of the immaterial universe. And we see them, on all sides, daily and hourly, refusing to enter it, sinking back into the ranks of the dwellers in physical life, clinging to the consciousnesses they have experienced and understand. The intellectual rejection of all purely spiritual knowledge is the most marked indication of this indolence, of which thinkers of every standing are certainly guilty.

That the initial effort is a heavy one is evident, and it is clearly a question of strength, as well as of willing activity. But there is no way of acquiring this strength, or of using it when acquired, except by the exercise of the will. It is vain to expect to be born into great possessions. In the kingdom of life there is no heredity except from the man's own past. He has to accumulate that which is his. This is evident to any observer of life who uses his eyes without blinding them by prejudice; and even when prejudice is present, it is impossible for a man of sense not to perceive the fact. It is from this that we get the doctrine of punishment and salvation, either lasting through great ages after death, or eternal. This doctrine is a narrow and unintelligent mode of stating the fact in Nature that what a man sows that shall he reap. Swedenborg's great mind saw the fact so clearly that he hardened it into a finality in reference to this particular existence, his prejudices making it impossible for him to perceive the possibility of new action when there is no longer the sensuous world to act in. He was too dogmatic for scientific observation, and would not see that, as the spring follows the autumn, and the day the night, so birth must follow death. He went very near the threshold of the Gates of Gold, and passed beyond mere intellectualism, only to pause at a point but one step farther. The glimpse of the life beyond which he had obtained appeared to him to contain the universe; and on his fragment of experience he built up a theory to include all life, and refused progress beyond that state or any possibility outside it. This is only another form of the weary treadmill. But Swedenborg stands foremost in the crowd of witnesses to the fact that the Golden Gates exist and can be seen from the heights of thought, and he has cast us a faint surge of sensation from their threshold.

III

When once one has considered the meaning of those Gates, it is evident that there is no other way out of this form of life except through them. They only can admit man to the place where he becomes the fruit of which manhood is the blossom. Nature is the kindest of mothers to those who need her; she never wearies of her children or desires them to lessen in multitude. Her friendly arms open wide to

the vast throng who desire birth and to dwell
in forms; and while they continue to desire
it, she continues to smile a welcome. Why,
then, should she shut her doors on any? When
one life in her heart has not worn out a hun-
dredth part of the soul's longing for sensation
such as it finds there, what reason can there
be for its departure to any other place? Surely
the seeds of desire spring up where the sower
has sown them. This seems but reasonable; and
on this apparently self-evident fact the Indian
mind has based its theory of re-incarnation, of
birth and re-birth in matter, which has become
so familiar a part of Eastern thought as no
longer to need demonstration. The Indian
knows it as the Western knows that the day
he is living through is but one of many days
which make up the span of a man's life. This
certainty which is possessed by the Eastern with
regard to natural laws that control the great
sweep of the soul's existence is simply acquired
by habits of thought. The mind of many is
fixed on subjects which in the West are considered unthinkable. Thus it is that the East

has produced the great flowers of the spiritual growth of humanity. On the mental steps of a million men Buddha passed through the Gates of Gold; and because a great crowd pressed about the threshold he was able to leave behind him words which prove that those Gates will open.

CHAPTER III

I

It is very easily seen that there is no one point in a man's life or experience where he is nearer the soul of things than at any other. That soul, the sublime essence, which fills the air with a burnished glow, is there, behind the Gates it colors with itself. But that there is no one pathway to it is immediately perceived from the fact that this soul must from its very nature be universal. The Gates of Gold do not admit to any special place; what they do is to open for egress from a special place. Man passes through them when he casts off his limitation. He may burst the shell that holds him in darkness, tear the veil that hides him from the eternal, at any point where it is easiest for him to do so; and most often this point will be where he least expects to find it. Men go in search of escape with the help of their minds, and lay down arbitrary and limited

[39]

laws as to how to attain the, to them, unattainable. Many, indeed, have hoped to pass through by the way of religion, and instead they have formed a place of thought and feeling so marked and fixed that it seems as though long ages would be insufficient to enable them to get out of the rut. Some have believed that by the aid of pure intellect a way was to be found; and to such men we owe the philosophy and metaphysics which have prevented the race from sinking into utter sensuousness. But the end of the man who endeavors to live by thought alone is that he dwells in fantasies, and insists on giving them to other men as substantial food. Great is our debt to the metaphysicians and transcendentalists; but he who follows them to the bitter end, forgetting that the brain is only one organ of use, will find himself dwelling in a place where a dull wheel of argument seems to turn forever on its axis, yet goes nowhither and carries no burden.

Virtue (or what seems to each man to be virtue, his own special standard of morality and purity) is held by those who practise it to be a way to heaven. Perhaps it is, to the heaven of the modern sybarite, the ethical voluptuary. It is as easy to become a gourmand in pure living and high thinking as in the pleasures of taste or sight or sound. Gratification is the aim of the virtuous man as well as of the drunkard; even if his life be a miracle of abstinence and self-sacrifice, a moment's thought shows that in pursuing this apparently heroic path he does but pursue pleasure. With him pleasure takes on a lovely form because his gratifications are those of a sweet savor, and it pleases him to give gladness to others rather than to enjoy himself at their expense. But the pure life and high thoughts are no more finalities in themselves than any other mode of enjoyment; and the man who endeavors to find contentment in them must intensify his effort and continually repeat it, — all in vain. He is a green plant indeed, and the leaves are beautiful; but more is wanted than leaves. If he persists in his endeavor blindly, believing that he has reached his goal when he has not even perceived it, then he finds himself in that dreary place where good is done perforce, and the deed of virtue is without the love that should shine through it. It is well for a man to lead a pure life, as it is well for him to have clean hands, — else he becomes repugnant. But virtue as we understand it now can no more have any special relation to the state beyond that to which we are limited than any other part of our constitution. Spirit is not a gas created by matter, and we cannot create our future by forcibly using one material agent and leaving out the rest. Spirit is the great life on which matter rests, as does the rocky world on the free and fluid ether; whenever we can break our limitations we find ourselves on that marvellous shore where Wordsworth once saw the gleam of the gold. When we enter there all the present must disappear alike, — virtue and vice, thought and sense. That a man reaps what he has sown must of course be true also; he has no power to carry virtue, which is of the material life, with him; yet the aroma of his good deeds is a far sweeter sacrifice than the odor of crime and cruelty. Yet it may be, however, that by the practice of virtue he will fetter himself into one groove, one changeless fashion of life in matter, so firmly that it is impossible for the mind to conceive that death is a sufficient power to free him, and cast him upon the broad and glorious ocean, — a sufficient power to undo for him the inexorable and heavy latch of the Golden Gate. And sometimes the man who has sinned so deeply that his whole nature is scarred and blackened by the fierce fire of selfish gratification is at last so utterly burned out and charred that from the very vigor of the passion light leaps forth. It would seem more possible for such a man at least to reach the threshold of the Gates than for the mere ascetic or philosopher.

But it is little use to reach the threshold of the Gates without the power to pass through. And that is all that the sinner can hope to do by the dissolution of himself which comes from seeing his own soul. At least this appears to be so, inevitably because his condition is negative. The man who lifts the latch of the

[43]

Golden Gate must do so with his own strong
hand, must be absolutely positive. This we can
see by analogy. In everything else in life, in
every new step or development, it is necessary
for a man to exercise his most dominant will
in order to obtain it fully. Indeed in many
cases, though he has every advantage and
though he use his will to some extent, he will
fail utterly of obtaining what he desires from
lack of the final and unconquerable resolution.
No education in the world will make a man
an intellectual glory to his age, even if his
powers are great; for unless he positively
desires to seize the flower of perfection, he will
be but a dry scholar, a dealer in words, a pro-
ficient in mechanical thought, and a mere wheel
of memory. And the man who has this positive
quality in him will rise in spite of adverse cir
cumstances, will recognize and seize upon the
tide of thought which is his natural food, and
will stand as a giant at last in the place he
willed to reach. We see this practically every
day in all walks of life. Wherefore it does not
seem possible that the man who has simply

succeeded through the passions in wrecking the dogmatic and narrow part of his nature should pass through those great Gates. But as he is not blinded by prejudice, nor has fastened himself to any treadmill of thought, nor caught the wheel of his soul in any deep rut of life, it would seem that if once the positive will might be born within him, he could at some time not hopelessly far distant lift his hand to the latch.

Undoubtedly it is the hardest task we have yet seen set us in life, that which we are now talking of, — to free a man of all prejudice, of all crystallized thought or feeling, of all limitations, yet develop within him the positive will. It seems too much of a miracle; for in ordinary life positive will is always associated with crystallized ideas. But many things which have appeared to be too much of a miracle for accomplishment have yet been done, even in the narrow experience of life given to our present humanity. All the past shows us that difficulty is no excuse for dejection, much less for despair; else the world would have been without the many wonders of civilization. Let us consider the thing more seriously, therefore, having once used our minds to the idea that it is not impossible.

The great initial difficulty is that of fastening the interest on that which is unseen. Yet this is done every day, and we have only to observe how it is done in order to guide our own conduct. Every inventor fastens his interest firmly on the unseen; and it entirely depends on the firmness of that attachment whether he is successful or whether he fails. The poet who looks on to his moment of creation as that for which he lives, sees that which is invisible and hears that which is soundless.

Probably in this last analogy there is a clew as to the mode by which success in this voyage to the unknown bourn ("whence," indeed, "no traveller returns") is attained. It applies also to the inventor and to all who reach out beyond the ordinary mental and psychical level of humanity. The clew lies in that word "creation."

II

The words "to create" are often understood
by the ordinary mind to convey the idea of
evolving something out of nothing. This is
clearly not its meaning; we are mentally obliged
to provide our Creator with chaos from which
to produce the worlds. The tiller of the soil,
who is the typical producer of social life, must
have his material, his earth, his sky, rain, and
sun, and the seeds to place within the earth.
Out of nothing he can produce nothing. Out
of a void Nature cannot arise; there is that
material beyond, behind, or within, from which
she is shaped by our desire for a universe. It
is an evident fact that the seeds and the earth,
air, and water which cause them to germinate
exist on every plane of action. If you talk to
an inventor, you will find that far ahead of
what he is now doing he can always perceive
some other thing to be done which he cannot
express in words because as yet he has not

drawn it into our present world of objects. That knowledge of the unseen is even more definite in the poet, and more inexpressible until he has touched it with some part of that consciousness which he shares with other men. But in strict proportion to his greatness he lives in the consciousness which the ordinary man does not even believe can exist, — the consciousness which dwells in the greater universe, which breathes in the vaster air, which beholds a wider earth and sky, and snatches seeds from plants of giant growth.

It is this place of consciousness that we need to reach out to. That it is not reserved only for men of genius is shown by the fact that martyrs and heroes have found it and dwelt in it. It is not reserved for men of genius only, but it can only be found by men of great soul.

In this fact there is no need for discouragement. Greatness in man is popularly supposed to be a thing inborn. This belief must be a result of want of thought, of blindness to facts of nature. Greatness can only be attained by growth; that is continually demonstrated to us. Even the mountains, even the firm globe itself, these are great by dint of the mode of growth peculiar to that state of materiality, — accumulation of atoms. As the consciousness inherent in all existing forms passes into more advanced forms of life it becomes more active, and in proportion it acquires the power of growth by assimilation instead of accumulation. Looking at existence from this special point of view (which indeed is a difficult one to maintain for long, as we habitually look at life in planes and forget the great lines which connect and run through these), we immediately perceive it to be reasonable to suppose that as we advance beyond our present standpoint the power of growth by assimilation will become greater and probably change into a method yet more rapid, easy, and unconscious. The universe is, in fact, full of magnificent promise for us, if we will but lift our eyes and see. It is that lifting of the eyes which is the first need and the first difficulty; we are so apt readily to be content with

[49]

what we see within touch of our hands. It is
the essential characteristic of the man of genius
that he is comparatively indifferent to that
fruit which is just within touch, and hungers
for that which is afar on the hills. In fact
he does not need the sense of contact to arouse
longing. He knows that this distant fruit,
which he perceives without the aid of the
physical senses, is a subtler and a stronger
food than any which appeals to them. And
how is he rewarded! When he tastes that
fruit, how strong and sweet is its flavor, and
what a new sense of life rushes upon him!
For in recognizing that flavor he has recognized the existence of the subtile senses, those
which feed the life of the inner man; and it is
by the strength of that inner man, and by his
strength only, that the latch of the Golden
Gates can be lifted.

In fact it is only by the development and
growth of the inner man that the existence
of these Gates, and of that to which they
admit, can be even perceived. While man is
content with his gross senses and cares nothing

for his subtile ones, the Gates remain literally invisible. As to the boor the gateway of the intellectual life is as a thing uncreate and non-existent, so to the man of the gross senses, even if his intellectual life is active, that which lies beyond is uncreate and non-existent, only because he does not open the book.

To the servant who dusts the scholar's library the closed volumes are meaningless; they do not even appear to contain a promise unless he also is a scholar, not merely a servant. It is possible to gaze throughout eternity upon a shut exterior from sheer indolence, — mental indolence, which is incredulity, and which at last men learn to pride themselves on; they call it scepticism, and talk of the reign of reason. It is no more a state to justify pride than that of the Eastern sybarite who will not even lift his food to his mouth; he is "reasonable" also in that he sees no value in activity, and therefore does not exercise it. So with the sceptic; decay follows the condition of inaction, whether it be mental, psychic, or physical.

III

And now let us consider how the initial difficulty of fastening the interest on that which is unseen is to be overcome. Our gross senses refer only to that which is objective in the ordinary sense of the word; but just beyond this field of life there are finer sensations which appeal to finer senses. Here we find the first clew to the stepping-stones we need. Man looks from this point of view like a point where many rays or lines center; and if he has the courage or the interest to detach himself from the simplest form of life, the point, and explore but a little way along these lines or rays, his whole being at once inevitably widens and expands, the man begins to grow in greatness. But it is evident, if we accept this illustration as a fairly true one, that the chief point of importance is to explore no more persistently on one line than another; else the result must be a deformity. We all know how powerful is the majesty and personal dignity of a forest tree which has had air enough to breathe, and room for its widening roots, and inner vitality with which to accomplish its unceasing task. It obeys the perfect natural law of growth, and the peculiar awe it inspires arises from this fact.

How is it possible to obtain recognition of the inner man, to observe its growth and foster it?

Let us try to follow a little way the clew we have obtained, though words will probably soon be useless.

We must each travel alone and without aids, as the traveller has to climb alone when he nears the summit of the mountain. No beast of burden can help him there; neither can the gross senses or anything that touches the gross senses help him here. But for a little distance words may go with us.

The tongue recognizes the value of sweetness or piquancy in food. To the man whose senses are of the simplest order there is no other idea of sweetness than this. But a finer essence, a more highly placed sensation of the same order, is reached by another perception.

[53]

The sweetness on the face of a lovely woman, or in the smile of a friend, is recognized by the man whose inner senses have even a little — a mere stirring of — vitality. To the one who has lifted the golden latch the spring of sweet waters, the fountain itself whence all softness arises, is opened and becomes part of his heritage.

But before this fountain can be tasted, or any other spring reached, any source found, a heavy weight has to be lifted from the heart, an iron bar which holds it down and prevents it from arising in its strength.

The man who recognizes the flow of sweetness from its source through Nature, through all forms of life, he has lifted this, he has raised himself into that state in which there is no bondage. He knows that he is a part of the great whole, and it is this knowledge which is his heritage. It is through the breaking asunder of the arbitrary bond which holds him to his personal center that he comes of age and becomes ruler of his kingdom. As he widens out, reaching by manifold experience

[54]

along those lines which center at the point where he stands embodied, he discovers that he has touch with all life, that he contains within himself the whole. And then he has but to yield himself to the great force which we call good, to clasp it tightly with the grasp of his soul, and he is carried swiftly on to the great, wide waters of real living. What are those waters? In our present life we have but the shadow of the substance. No man loves without satiety, no man drinks wine without return of thirst. Hunger and longing darken the sky and make the earth unfriendly. What we need is an earth that will bear living fruit, a sky that will be always full of light. Needing this positively, we shall surely find it.

CHAPTER IV

THE MEANING OF PAIN

I

LOOK into the deep heart of life, whence pain comes to darken men's lives. She is always on the threshold, and behind her stands despair.

What are these two gaunt figures, and why are they permitted to be our constant followers?

It is we who permit them, we who order them, as we permit and order the action of our bodies; and we do so as unconsciously. But by scientific experiment and investigation we have learned much about our physical life, and it would seem as if we can obtain at least as much result with regard to our inner life by adopting similar methods.

Pain arouses, softens, breaks, and destroys. Regarded from a sufficiently removed standpoint, it appears as medicine, as a knife, as a weapon, as a poison, in turn. It is an implement, a thing which is used, evidently. What we desire to discover is, who is the user; what part of ourselves is it that demands the presence of this thing so hateful to the rest?

Medicine is used by the physician, the knife by the surgeon; but the weapon of destruction is used by the enemy, the hater.

Is it, then, that we do not only use means, or desire to use means, for the benefit of our souls, but that also we wage warfare within ourselves, and do battle in the inner sanctuary? It would seem so; for it is certain that if man's will relaxed with regard to it he would no longer retain life in that state in which pain exists. Why does he desire his own hurt?

The answer may at first sight seem to be that he primarily desires pleasure, and so is willing to continue on that battlefield where it wages war with pain for the possession of him, hoping always that pleasure will win the victory and take him home to herself. This is but the external aspect of the man's state. In himself he knows well that pain is co-ruler with pleasure, and that though the war wages always it never will be won. The superficial observer concludes that man submits to the inevitable. But that is a fallacy not worthy of discussion. A little serious thought shows us that man does not exist at all except by exercise of his positive qualities; it is but logical to suppose that he chooses the state he will live in by the exercise of those same qualities.

Granted, then, for the sake of our argument, that he desires pain, why is it that he desires anything so annoying to himself?

II

If we carefully consider the constitution of man and its tendencies, it would seem as if there were two definite directions in which he grows. He is like a tree which strikes its roots into the ground while it throws up young branches towards the heavens. These two lines which go outward from the central personal point are to him clear, definite, and intelligible. He calls one good and the other evil. But man is not, according to any analogy, observation, or experience, a straight line. Would that he were, and that life, or progress, or development, or whatever we choose to call it, meant merely following one straight road or another, as the religionists pretend it does. The whole question, the mighty problem, would be very easily solved then. But it is not so easy to go to hell as preachers declare it to be. It is as hard a task as to find one's way to the Golden Gate. A man may wreck himself utterly in sense-pleasure, — may debase his whole nature, as it seems, — yet he fails of becoming the perfect devil, for there is still the spark of divine light within him. He tries to choose the broad road which leads to destruction, and enters bravely on his headlong career. But very soon he is checked and startled by some unthought-of tendency in himself, — some of the many other radiations which go forth from his center of self. He suffers as the body suffers when it develops monstrosities which impede its healthy action. He has created pain, and encountered his own creation. It may seem as if this argument is difficult of application with regard to physical pain. Not so, if man is regarded from a loftier standpoint than that we generally occupy. If he is looked upon as a powerful consciousness which forms its external manifestations according to its desires, then it is evident that physical pain results from deformity in those desires. No doubt it will appear to many minds that this conception of man is too gratuitous, and involves too large a mental leap into unknown places where proof is unobtainable. But if the mind is accustomed to look upon life from this standpoint, then very soon none other is acceptable; the threads of existence, which to the purely materialistic observer appear hopelessly entangled, become separated and straightened, so that a new intelligibleness illumines the universe. The arbitrary and cruel Creator who inflicts pain and pleasure at will then disappears from the stage; and it is well, for he is indeed an unnecessary character, and, worse still, is a mere creature of straw, who cannot even strut upon the boards without being upheld on all sides by dogmatists. Man

[60]

comes into this world, surely, on the same principle that he lives in one city of the earth or another; at all events, if it is too much to say that this is so, one may safely ask, why is it not so? There is neither for nor against which will appeal to the materialist, or which would weigh in a court of justice; but I aver this in favor of the argument, — that no man having once seriously considered it can go back to the formal theories of the sceptics. It is like putting on swaddling-clothes again.

Granting, then, for the sake of this argument, that man is a powerful consciousness who is his own creator, his own judge, and within whom lies all life in potentiality, even the ultimate goal, then let us consider why he causes himself to suffer.

If pain is the result of uneven development, of monstrous growths, of defective advance at different points, why does man not learn the lesson which this should teach him, and take pains to develop equally?

It would seem to me as if the answer to this question is that this is the very lesson which the human race is engaged in learning. Perhaps this may seem too bold a statement to make in the face of ordinary thinking, which either regards man as a creature of chance dwelling in chaos, or as a soul bound to the inexorable wheel of a tyrant's chariot and hurried on either to heaven or to hell. But such a mode of thought is after all but the same as that of the child who regards his parents as the final arbiters of his destinies, and in fact the gods or demons of his universe. As he grows he casts aside this idea, finding that it is simply a question of coming of age, and that he is himself the king of life like any other man.

So it is with the human race. It is king of its world, arbiter of its own destiny, and there is none to say it nay. Who talk of Providence and chance have not paused to think.

Destiny, the inevitable, does indeed exist for the race and for the individual; but who can ordain this save the man himself? There is no clew in heaven or earth to the existence of any ordainer other than the man who suffers

or enjoys that which is ordained. We know
so little of our own constitution, we are so
ignorant of our divine functions, that it is
impossible for us yet to know how much or
how little we are actually fate itself. But this
at all events we know, — that so far as any
provable perception goes, no clew to the
existence of an ordainer has yet been discovered; whereas if we give but a very little
attention to the life about us in order to
observe the action of the man upon his own
future, we soon perceive this power as an
actual force in operation. It is visible, although
our range of vision is so very limited.

The man of the world, pure and simple,
is by far the best practical observer and
philosopher with regard to life, because he is
not blinded by any prejudices. He will be
found always to believe that as a man sows so
shall he reap. And this is so evidently true
when it is considered, that if one takes the
larger view, including all human life, it makes
intelligible the awful Nemesis which seems
consciously to pursue the human race, — that

inexorable appearance of pain in the midst of pleasure. The great Greek poets saw this apparition so plainly that their recorded observation has given to us younger and blinder observers the idea of it. It is unlikely that so materialistic a race as that which has grown up all over the West would have discovered for itself the existence of this terrible factor in human life without the assistance of the older poets, — the poets of the past. And in this we may notice, by the way, one distinct value of the study of the classics, — that the great ideas and facts about human life which the superb ancients put into their poetry shall not be absolutely lost as are their arts. No doubt the world will flower again, and greater thoughts and more profound discoveries than those of the past will be the glory of the men of the future efflorescence; but until that far-off day comes we cannot prize too dearly the treasures left us.

There is one aspect of the question which seems at first sight positively to negative this mode of thought; and that is the suffering in the apparently purely physical body of the dumb beings, — young children, idiots, animals, — and their desperate need of the power which comes of any sort of knowledge to help them through their sufferings.

The difficulty which will arise in the mind with regard to this comes from the untenable idea of the separation of the soul from the body. It is supposed by all those who look only at material life (and especially by the physicians of the flesh) that the body and the brain are a pair of partners who live together hand in hand and react one upon another. Beyond that they recognize no cause and therefore allow of none. They forget that the brain and the body are as evidently mere mechanism as the hand or the foot. There is the inner man — the soul — behind, using all these mechanisms; and this is as evidently the truth with regard to all the existences we know of as with regard to man himself. We cannot find any point in the scale of being at which soul-causation ceases or can cease. The dull oyster must have that in him which makes him choose the inactive life he leads; none else can choose it for him but the soul behind, which makes him be. How else can he be where he is, or be at all? Only by the intervention of an impossible creator called by some name or other.

It is because man is so idle, so indisposed to assume or accept responsibility, that he falls back upon this temporary makeshift of a creator. It is temporary indeed, for it can only last during the activity of the particular brain power which finds its place among us. When the man drops this mental life behind him, he of necessity leaves with it its magic lantern and the pleasant illusions he has conjured up by its aid. That must be a very uncomfortable moment, and must produce a sense of nakedness not to be approached by any other sensation. It would seem as well to save one's self this disagreeable experience by refusing to accept unreal phantasms as things of flesh and blood and power. Upon the shoulders of the Creator man likes to thrust the responsibility not only of his capacity for sinning and the possibility of his salvation, but of his very

life itself, his very consciousness. It is a poor
Creator that he thus contents himself with, —
one who is pleased with a universe of puppets,
and amused by pulling their strings. If he is
capable of such enjoyment, he must yet be in
his infancy. Perhaps that is so, after all; the
God within us is in his infancy, and refuses
to recognize his high estate. If indeed the soul
of man is subject to the laws of growth, of
decay, and of re-birth as to its body, then there
is no wonder at its blindness. But this is
evidently not so; for the soul of man is of that
order of life which causes shape and form,
and is unaffected itself by these things, — of
that order of life which like the pure, the
abstract flame burns wherever it is lit. This
cannot be changed or affected by time, and is
of its very nature superior to growth and
decay. It stands in that primeval place which
is the only throne of God, — that place whence
forms of life emerge and to which they return.
That place is the central point of existence,
where there is a permanent spot of life as
there is in the midst of the heart of man. It

is by the equal development of that, — first
by the recognition of it, and then by its equal
development upon the many radiating lines of
experience, — that man is at last enabled to
reach the Golden Gate and lift the latch. The
process is the gradual recognition of the god
in himself; the goal is reached when that
godhood is consciously restored to its right
glory.

III

The first thing which it is necessary for the
soul of man to do in order to engage in this
great endeavor of discovering true life is the
same thing that the child first does in its desire
for activity in the body, — he must be able to
stand. It is clear that the power of standing,
of equilibrium, of concentration, of upright-
ness, in the soul, is a quality of a marked character. The word that presents itself most
readily as descriptive of this quality is
"confidence."

To remain still amid life and its changes,
and stand firmly on the chosen spot, is a feat

which can only be accomplished by the man who has confidence in himself and in his destiny. Otherwise the hurrying forms of life, the rushing tide of men, the great floods of thought, must inevitably carry him with them, and then he will lose that place of consciousness whence it was possible to start on the great enterprise. For it *must* be done knowingly, and without pressure from without, — this act of the new-born man. All the great ones of the earth have possessed this confidence, and have stood firmly on that place which was to them the one solid spot in the universe. To each man this place is of necessity different. Each man must find his own earth and his own heaven.

We have the instinctive desire to relieve pain, but we work in externals in this as in everything else. We simply alleviate it; and if we do more, and drive it from its first chosen stronghold, it reappears in some other place with reinforced vigor. If it is eventually driven off the physical plane by persistent and successful effort, it reappears on the mental or emotional planes where no man can touch it. That this is so is easily seen by those who connect the various planes of sensation, and who observe life with that additional illumination. Men habitually regard these different forms of feeling as actually separate, whereas in fact they are evidently only different sides of one center, — the point of personality. If that which arises in the center, the fount of life, demands some hindered action, and consequently causes pain, the force thus created being driven from one stronghold must find another; it cannot be driven out. And all the blendings of human life which cause emotion and distress exist for its use and purposes as well as for those of pleasure. Both have their home in man; both demand their expression of right. The marvellously delicate mechanism of the human frame is constructed to answer to their lightest touch; the extraordinary intricacies of human relations evolve themselves, as it were, for the satisfaction of these two great opposites of the soul.

Pain and pleasure stand apart and separate,

as do the two sexes; and it is in the merging, the making the two into one, that joy and deep sensation and profound peace are obtained. Where there is neither male nor female, neither pain nor pleasure, there is the god in man dominant, and then is life real.

To state the matter in this way may savor too much of the dogmatist who utters his assertions uncontradicted from a safe pulpit; but it is dogmatism only as a scientist's record of effort in a new direction is dogmatism. Unless the existence of the Gates of Gold can be proved to be real, and not the mere phantasmagoria of fanciful visionaries, then they are not worth talking about at all. In the nineteenth century hard facts or legitimate arguments alone appeal to men's minds; and so much the better. For unless the life we advance towards is increasingly real and actual, it is worthless, and time is wasted in going after it. Reality is man's greatest need, and he demands to have it at all hazards, at any price. Be it so. No one doubts he is right. Let us then go in search of reality.

[71]

IV

One definite lesson learned by all acute sufferers will be of the greatest service to us in this consideration. In intense pain a point is reached where it is indistinguishable from its opposite, pleasure. This is indeed so, but few have the heroism or the strength to suffer to such a far point. It is as difficult to reach it by the other road. Only a chosen few have the gigantic capacity for pleasure which will enable them to travel to its other side. Most have but enough strength to enjoy and to become the slave of the enjoyment. Yet man has undoubtedly within himself the heroism needed for the great journey; else how is it that martyrs have smiled amid the torture? How is it that the profound sinner who lives for pleasure can at last feel stir within himself the divine afflatus?

In both these cases the possibility has arisen of finding the way; but too often that possibility is killed by the overbalance of the startled nature. The martyr has acquired a passion for pain and lives in the idea of heroic suffering; the sinner becomes blinded by the thought of virtue and worships it as an end, an object, a thing divine in itself; whereas it can only be divine as it is part of that infinite whole which includes vice as well as virtue. How is it possible to divide the infinite, — that which is one? It is as reasonable to lend divinity to any object as to take a cup of water from the sea and declare that in that is contained the ocean. You cannot separate the ocean; the salt water is part of the great sea and must be so; but nevertheless you do not hold the sea in your hand. Men so longingly desire personal power that they are ready to put infinity into a cup, the divine idea into a formula, in order that they may fancy themselves in possession of it. These only are those who cannot rise and approach the Gates of Gold, for the great breath of life confuses them; they are struck with horror to find how great it is. The idol-worshipper keeps an image of his idol in his heart and burns a candle always before it. It is his own, and he is pleased at that thought, even if he bow in reverence before it. In how many virtuous and religious men does not this same state exist? In the recesses of the soul the lamp is burning before a household god, — a thing possessed by its worshipper and subject to him. Men cling with desperate tenacity to these dogmas, these moral laws, these principles and modes of faith which are their household gods, their personal idols. Bid them burn the unceasing flame in reverence only to the infinite, and they turn from you. Whatever their manner of scorning your protest may be, within themselves it leaves a sense of aching void. For the noble soul of the man, that potential king which is within us all, knows full well that this household idol may be cast down and destroyed at any moment, — that it is without finality in itself, without any real and absolute life. And he has been content in his possession, forgetting that anything possessed can only by the immutable laws of life be held temporarily. He has forgotten that the infinite is his only friend; he has forgotten that in its

[74]

glory is his only home, — that it alone can be his god. There he feels as if he is homeless; but that amid the sacrifices he offers to his own especial idol there is for him a brief resting-place; and for this he clings passionately to it.

Few have the courage even slowly to face the great desolateness which lies outside themselves, and must lie there so long as they cling to the person which they represent, the "I" which is to them the center of the world, the cause of all life. In their longing for a God they find the reason for the existence of one; in their desire for a sense-body and a world to enjoy in, lies to them the cause of the universe. These beliefs may be hidden very deep beneath the surface, and be indeed scarcely accessible; but in the fact that they are there is the reason why the man holds himself upright. To himself he is himself the infinite and the God; he holds the ocean in a cup. In this delusion he nurtures the egoism which makes life pleasure and makes pain pleasant. In this profound egoism is the very cause and source of the existence of pleasure and of pain. For unless man vacillated between these two, and ceaselessly reminded himself by sensation that he exists, he would forget it. And in this fact lies the whole answer to the question, "Why does man create pain for his own discomfort?"

The strange and mysterious fact remains unexplained as yet, that man in so deluding himself is merely interpreting Nature backwards and putting into the words of death the meaning of life. For that man does indeed hold within him the infinite, and that the ocean is really in the cup, is an incontestable truth; but it is only so because the cup is absolutely non-existent. It is merely an experience of the infinite, having no permanence, liable to be shattered at any instant. It is in the claiming of reality and permanence for the four walls of his personality, that man makes the vast blunder which plunges him into a prolonged series of unfortunate incidents, and intensifies continually the existence of his favorite forms of sensation. Pleasure and pain become to him more real than the great ocean of which he is a part and where his home is; he perpetually knocks himself painfully against these walls where he feels, and his tiny self oscillates within his chosen prison.

CHAPTER V

I

STRENGTH to step forward is the primary need of him who has chosen his path. Where is this to be found? Looking round, it is not hard to see where other men find their strength. Its source is profound conviction. Through this great moral power is brought to birth in the natural life of the man that which enables him, however frail he may be, to go on and conquer. Conquer what? Not continents, not worlds, but himself. Through that supreme victory is obtained the entrance to the whole, where all that might be conquered and obtained by effort becomes at once not his, but himself.

To put on armor and go forth to war, taking the chances of death in the hurry of the fight, is an easy thing; to stand still amid the jangle of the world, to preserve stillness within the turmoil of the body, to hold silence amid the thousand cries of the senses and

[78]

desires, and then, stripped of all armor and without hurry or excitement take the deadly serpent of self and kill it, is no easy thing. Yet that is what has to be done; and it can only be done in the moment of equilibrium when the enemy is disconcerted by the silence.

But there is needed for this supreme moment a strength such as no hero of the battlefield needs. A great soldier must be filled with the profound convictions of the justness of his cause and the rightness of his method. The man who wars against himself and wins the battle can do it only when he knows that in that war he is doing the one thing which is worth doing, and when he knows that in doing it he is winning heaven and hell as his servitors. Yes, he stands on both. He needs no heaven where pleasure comes as a long-promised reward; he fears no hell where pain waits to punish him for his sins. For he has conquered once for all that shifting serpent in himself which turns from side to side in its constant desire of contact, in its perpetual search after pleasure and pain. Never again

[79]

(the victory once really won) can he tremble or grow exultant at any thought of that which the future holds. Those burning sensations which seemed to him to be the only proofs of his existence are his no longer. How, then, can he know that he lives? He knows it only by argument. And in time he does not care to argue about it. For him there is then peace; and he will find in that peace the power he has coveted. Then he will know what is that faith which can remove mountains.

II

Religion holds a man back from the path, prevents his stepping forward, for various very plain reasons. First, it makes the vital mistake of distinguishing between good and evil. Nature knows no such distinction; and the moral and social laws set us by our religions are as temporary, as much a thing of our own special mode and form of existence, as are the moral and social laws of the ants or the bees. We pass out of that state in which these things appear to be final, and we forget them forever. This is easily shown, because a man of broad habits of thought and of intelligence must modify his code of life when he dwells among another people. These people among whom he is an alien have their own deep-rooted religions and hereditary convictions, against which he cannot offend. Unless his is an abjectly narrow and unthinking mind, he sees that their form of law and order is as good as his own. What then can he do but reconcile his conduct gradually to their rules? And then if he dwells among them many years the sharp edge of difference is worn away, and he forgets at last where their faith ends and his commences. Yet is it for his own people to say he has done wrong, if he has injured no man and remained just?

I am not attacking law and order; I do not speak of these things with rash dislike. In their place they are as vital and necessary as the code which governs the life of a beehive is to its successful conduct. What I wish to point out is that law and order in themselves are quite temporary and unsatisfactory. When a man's soul passes away from its brief dwelling-place, thoughts of law and order do not accompany it. If it is strong, it is the ecstasy of true being and real life which it becomes possessed of, as all know who have watched by the dying. If the soul is weak, it faints and fades away, overcome by the first flush of the new life.

Am I speaking too positively? Only those who live in the active life of the moment, who have not watched beside the dead and dying, who have not walked the battlefield and looked in the faces of men in their last agony, will say so. The strong man goes forth from his body exultant.

Why? Because he is no longer held back and made to quiver by hesitation. In the strange moment of death he has had release given him; and with a sudden passion of delight he recognizes that it is release. Had he been sure of this before, he would have been a great sage, a man to rule the world, for he would have had the power to rule

[82]

himself and his own body. That release from the chains of ordinary life can be obtained as easily during life as by death. It only needs a sufficiently profound conviction to enable the man to look on his body with the same emotions as he would look on the body of another man, or on the bodies of a thousand men. In contemplating a battlefield it is impossible to realize the agony of every sufferer; why, then, realize your own pain more keenly than another's? Mass the whole together, and look at it all from a wider standpoint than that of the individual life. That you actually feel your own physical wound is a weakness of your limitation. The man who is developed psychically feels the wound of another as keenly as his own, and does not feel his own at all if he is strong enough to will it so. Every one who has examined at all seriously into psychic conditions knows this to be a fact, more or less marked, according to the psychic development. In many instances the psychic is more keenly and selfishly aware of his own pain than of any other person's; but that is when the development, marked perhaps so far as it has gone, only reaches a certain point. It is the power which carries the man to the margin of that consciousness which is profound peace and vital activity. It can carry him no further. But if he has reached its margin he is freed from the paltry dominion of his own self. That is the first great release. Look at the sufferings which come upon us from our narrow and limited experience and sympathy. We each stand quite alone, a solitary unit, a pygmy in the world. What good fortune can we expect? The great life of the world rushes by, and we are in danger each instant that it will overwhelm us or even utterly destroy us. There is no defence to be offered to it; no opposition army can be set up, because in this life every man fights his own battle against every other man, and no two can be united under the same banner. There is only one way of escape from this terrible danger which we battle against every hour. Turn round, and instead of standing against the forces, join them; become one with Nature, and go easily upon her path. Do not resist or resent the circumstances of life any more than the plants resent the rain and the wind. Then suddenly, to your own amazement, you find you have time and strength to spare, to use in the great battle which it is inevitable every man must fight, — that in himself, that which leads to his own conquest.

Some might say, to his own destruction. And why? Because from the hour when he first tastes the splendid reality of living he forgets more and more his individual self. No longer does he fight for it, or pit its strength against the strength of others. No longer does he care to defend or to feed it. Yet when he is thus indifferent to its welfare, the individual self grows more stalwart and robust, like the prairie grasses and the trees of untrodden forests. It is a matter of indifference to him whether this is so or not. Only, if it is so, he has a fine instrument ready to his hand; and in due proportion to the completeness of his indifference to it is the strength and beauty of his personal self. This is readily seen; a garden flower becomes a mere degenerate copy of itself if it is simply neglected; a plant must be cultivated to the highest pitch, and benefit by the whole of the gardener's skill, or else it must be a pure savage, wild, and fed only by the earth and sky. Who cares for any intermediate state? What value or strength is there in the neglected garden rose which has the canker in every bud? For diseased or dwarfed blossoms are sure to result from an arbitrary change of condition, resulting from the neglect of the man who has hitherto been the providence of the plant in its unnatural life. But there are wind-blown plains where the daisies grow tall, with moon faces such as no cultivation can produce in them. Cultivate, then, to the very utmost; forget no inch of your garden ground, no smallest plant that grows in it; make no foolish pretence nor fond mistake in the fancy that you are ready to forget it, and so subject it to the frightful consequences of half-measures. The plant that is watered today and forgotten tomorrow must dwindle or decay. The plant that looks for no

help but from Nature itself measures its
strength at once, and either dies and is
re-created or grows into a great tree whose
boughs fill the sky. But make no mistake like
the religionists and some philosophers; leave
no part of yourself neglected while you know
it to be yourself. While the ground is the
gardener's it is his business to tend it; but
some day a call may come to him from another
country or from death itself, and in a moment
he is no longer the gardener, his business is at
an end, he has no more duty of that kind
at all. Then his favorite plants suffer and die,
and the delicate ones become one with the
earth. But soon fierce Nature claims the place
for her own, and covers it with thick grass or
giant weeds, or nurses some sapling in it
till its branches shade the ground. Be warned,
and tend your garden to the utmost, till you can
pass away utterly and let it return to Nature
and become the wind-blown plain where the
wild-flowers grow. Then, if you pass that way
and look at it, whatever has happened will
neither grieve nor elate you. For you will be

able to say, "I am the rocky ground, I am the great tree, I am the strong daisies," indifferent which it is that flourishes where once your rose-trees grew. But you must have learned to study the stars to some purpose before you dare to neglect your roses, and omit to fill the air with their cultivated fragrance. You must know your way through the trackless air, and from thence to the pure ether; you must be ready to lift the bar of the Golden Gate.

Cultivate, I say, and neglect nothing. Only remember, all the while you tend and water, that you are impudently usurping the tasks of Nature herself. Having usurped her work, you must carry it through until you have reached a point when she has no power to punish you, when you are not afraid of her, but can with a bold front return her her own. She laughs in her sleeve, the mighty mother, watching you with covert, laughing eye, ready relentlessly to cast the whole of your work into the dust if you do but give her the chance, if you turn idler and grow careless. The idler is father of the madman in the sense that the child is the father of the man. Nature has put her vast hand on him and crushed the whole edifice. The gardener and his rose-trees are alike broken and stricken by the great storm which her movement has created; they lie helpless till the sand is swept over them and they are buried in a weary wilderness. From this desert spot Nature herself will re-create, and will use the ashes of the man who dared to face her as indifferently as the withered leaves of his plants. His body, soul, and spirit are all alike claimed by her.

III

The man who is strong, who has resolved to find the unknown path, takes with the utmost care every step. He utters no idle word, he does no unconsidered action, he neglects no duty or office however homely or however difficult. But while his eyes and hands and feet are thus fulfilling their tasks, new eyes and hands and feet are being born within him. For his passionate and unceasing desire is to go that way on which the subtile organs only can guide him. The physical world he has learned, and knows how to use; gradually his power is passing on, and he recognizes the psychic world. But he has to learn this world and know how to use it, and he dare not lose hold of the life he is familiar with till he has taken hold of that with which he is unfamiliar. When he has acquired such power with his psychic organs as the infant has with its physical organs when it first opens its lungs, then is the hour for the great adventure. How little is needed — yet how much that is! The man does but need the psychic body to be formed in all parts, as is an infant's; he does but need the profound and unshakable conviction which impels the infant, that the new life is desirable. Once those conditions gained and he may let himself live in the new atmosphere and look up to the new sun. But then he must remember to check his new experience by the old. He is breathing still, though differently; he draws air into his lungs, and takes life from the sun. He has been born into the psychic world, and depends now on the psychic air and light. His goal is not here: this is but a subtile repetition of physical life; he has to pass through it according to similar laws. He must study, learn, grow, and conquer; never forgetting the while that his goal is that place where there is no air nor any sun or moon.

Do not imagine that in this line of progress the man himself is being moved or changing his place. Not so. The truest illustration of the process is that of cutting through layers of crust or skin. The man, having learned his lesson fully, casts off the physical life; having learned his lesson fully, casts off the psychic life; having learned his lesson fully, casts off the contemplative life, or life of adoration.

All are cast aside at last, and he enters the great temple where any memory of self or sensation is left outside as the shoes are cast from the feet of the worshipper. That temple is the place of his own pure divinity, the central flame which, however obscured, has animated him through all these struggles. And having found this sublime home he is sure as the heavens themselves. He remains still, filled with all knowledge and power. The outer man, the adoring, the acting, the living personification, goes its own way hand in hand with Nature, and shows all the superb strength of the savage growth of the earth, lit by that instinct which contains knowledge. For in the inmost sanctuary, in the actual temple, the man has found the subtile essence of Nature herself. No longer can there be any difference between them or any half-measures. And now comes the hour of action and power. In that inmost sanctuary all is to be found: God and his creatures, the fiends who prey on them, those among men who have been loved, those who have been hated. Difference between them exists no longer. Then the soul of man laughs in its strength and fearlessness, and goes forth into the world in which its actions are needed, and causes these actions to take place without apprehension, alarm, fear, regret, or joy.

This state is possible to man while yet he

lives in the physical; for men have attained it while living. It alone can make actions in the physical divine and true.

Life among objects of sense must forever be an outer shape to the sublime soul, — it can only become powerful life, the life of accomplishment, when it is animated by the crowned and indifferent god that sits in the sanctuary.

The obtaining of this condition is so supremely desirable because from the moment it is entered there is no more trouble, no more anxiety, no more doubt or hesitation. As a great artist paints his picture fearlessly and never committing any error which causes him regret, so the man who has formed his inner self deals with his life.

But that is when the condition is entered. That which we who look towards the mountains hunger to know is the mode of entrance and the way to the Gate. The Gate is that Gate of Gold barred by a heavy bar of iron. The way to the threshold of it turns a man giddy and sick. It seems no path, it seems to end per-

[93]

petually, its way lies along hideous precipices, it loses itself in deep waters.

Once crossed and the way found it appears wonderful that the difficulty should have looked so great. For the path where it disappears does but turn abruptly, its line upon the precipice edge is wide enough for the feet, and across the deep waters that look so treacherous there is always a ford and a ferry. So it happens in all profound experiences of human nature. When the first grief tears the heart asunder it seems that the path has ended and a blank darkness taken the place of the sky. And yet by groping the soul passes on, and that difficult and seemingly hopeless turn in the road is passed.

So with many another form of human torture. Sometimes throughout a long period or a whole lifetime the path of existence is perpetually checked by what seem like insurmountable obstacles. Grief, pain, suffering, the loss of all that is beloved or valued, rise up before the terrified soul and check it at every turn. Who places those obstacles there? The reason shrinks at the childish dramatic picture which the religionists place before it, — God permitting the Devil to torment His creatures for their ultimate good! When will that ultimate good be attained? The idea involved in this picture supposes an end, a goal. There is none. We can any one of us safely assent to that; for as far as human observation, reason, thought, intellect, or instinct can reach towards grasping the mystery of life, all data obtained show that the path is endless and that eternity cannot be blinked and converted by the idling soul into a million years.

In man, taken individually or as a whole, there clearly exists a double constitution. I am speaking roughly now, being well aware that the various schools of philosophy cut him up and subdivide him according to their several theories. What I mean is this: that two great tides of emotion sweep through his nature, two great forces guide his life; the one makes him an animal, and the other makes him a god. No brute of the earth is so brutal as the man who subjects his godly power to his animal power.

[95]

This is a matter of course, because the whole
force of the double nature is then used in one
direction. The animal pure and simple obeys
his instincts only and desires no more than to
gratify his love of pleasure; he pays but little
regard to the existence of other beings except
in so far as they offer him pleasure or pain; he
knows nothing of the abstract love of cruelty or
of any of those vicious tendencies of the human
being which have in themselves their own
gratification. Thus the man who becomes a
beast has a million times the grasp of life over
the natural beast, and that which in the pure
animal is sufficiently innocent enjoyment, unin-
terrupted by an arbitrary moral standard, becomes in him vice, because it is gratified on
principle. Moreover he turns all the divine
powers of his being into this channel, and de-
grades his soul by making it the slave of his
senses. The god, deformed and disguised,
waits on the animal and feeds it.

Consider then whether it is not possible to
change the situation. The man himself is king
of the country in which this strange spectacle

is seen. He allows the beast to usurp the place
of the god because for the moment the beast
pleases his capricious royal fancy the most. This
cannot last always; why let it last any longer?
So long as the animal rules there will be the
keenest sufferings in consequence of change,
of the vibration between pleasure and pain,
of the desire for prolonged and pleasant
physical life. And the god in his capacity of
servant adds a thousand-fold to all this, by
making physical life so much more filled with
keenness of pleasure, — rare, voluptuous,
aesthetic pleasure, — and by intensity of pain
so passionate that one knows not where it
ends and where pleasure commences. So
long as the god serves, so long the life of
the animal will be enriched and increasingly
valuable. But let the king resolve to change
the face of his court and forcibly evict the animal from the chair of state, restoring the god
to the place of divinity.

Ah, the profound peace that falls upon the
palace! All is indeed changed. No longer is
there the fever of personal longings or desires,

no longer is there any rebellion or distress, no longer any hunger for pleasure or dread of pain. It is like a great calm descending on a stormy ocean; it is like the soft rain of summer falling on parched ground; it is like the deep pool found amidst the weary, thirsty labyrinths of the unfriendly forest.

But there is much more than this. Not only is man more than an animal because there is the god in him, but he is more than a god because there is the animal in him.

Once force the animal into his rightful place, that of the inferior, and you find yourself in possession of a great force hitherto unsuspected and unknown. The god as servant adds a thousand-fold to the pleasures of the animal; the animal as servant adds a thousand-fold to the powers of the god. And it is upon the union, the right relation of these two forces in himself, that man stands as a strong king, and is enabled to raise his hand and lift the bar of the Golden Gate. When these forces are unfitly related, then the king is but a crowned voluptuary, without power, and whose

[98]

dignity does but mock him; for the animals, undivine, at least know peace and are not torn by vice and despair.

That is the whole secret. That is what makes man strong, powerful, able to grasp heaven and earth in his hands. Do not fancy it is easily done. Do not be deluded into the idea that the religious or the virtuous man does it! Not so. They do no more than fix a standard, a routine, a law, by which they hold the animal in check. The god is compelled to serve him in a certain way, and does so, pleasing him with the beliefs and cherished fantasies of the religious, with the lofty sense of personal pride which makes the joy of the virtuous. These special and canonized vices are things too low and base to be possible to the pure animal, whose only inspirer is Nature herself, always fresh as the dawn. The god in man, degraded, is a thing unspeakable in its infamous power of production.

The animal in man, elevated, is a thing unimaginable in its great powers of service and of strength.

[99]

You forget, you who let your animal self live on, merely checked and held within certain bounds, that it is a great force, an integral portion of the animal life of the world you live in. With it you can sway men, and influence the very world itself, more or less perceptibly according to your strength. The god, given his right place, will so inspire and guide this extraordinary creature, so educate and develop it, so force it into action and recognition of its kind, that it will make you tremble when you recognize the power that has awakened within you. The animal in yourself will then be a king among the animals of the world.

This is the secret of the old-world magicians, who made Nature serve them and work miracles every day for their convenience. This is the secret of the coming race which Lord Lytton foreshadowed for us.

But this power can only be attained by giving the god the sovereignty. Make your animal ruler over yourself, and he will never rule others.

[100]

EPILOGUE

SECRETED and hidden in the heart of the world and in the heart of man is the light which can illumine all life, the future and the past. Shall we not search for it? Surely some must do so. And then perhaps those will add what is needed to this poor fragment of thought.

THROUGH THE GATES OF GOLD

From *The Path,* March, 1887

THE most notable book for guidance in Mysticism which has appeared since *Light on the Path* was written has just been published under the significant title of *Through the Gates of Gold.* Though the author's name is withheld, the occult student will quickly discern that it must proceed from a very high source. In certain respects the book may be regarded as a commentary on *Light on the Path.* The reader would do well to bear this in mind. Many things in that book will be made clear by the reading of this one, and one will be constantly reminded of that work, which has already become a classic in our literature. *Through the Gates of Gold* is a work to be kept constantly at hand for reference and study. It will surely take rank as one of the standard books of Theosophy.

The "Gates of Gold" represent the entrance to that realm of the soul unknowable through the physical perceptions, and the purpose of this work is to indicate some of the steps necessary to reach their threshold. Through its extraordinary beauty of style and the clearness of its statement it will appeal to a wider portion of the public than most works of a Theosophical character. It speaks to the Western World in its own language, and in this fact lies much of its value.

Those of us who have been longing for something "practical" will find it here, while it will probably come into the hands of thousands who know little or nothing of Theosophy, and thus meet wants deeply felt though unexpressed. There are also doubtless many, we fancy, who will be carried far along in its pages by its resistless logic until they encounter something which will give a rude shock to some of their old conceptions, which they have imagined as firmly based as upon a rock — a shock which may cause them to draw back in alarm, but from which they will not find it so easy to recover, and which will be likely to set them thinking seriously.

The titles of the five chapters of the book are, respectively, "The Search for Pleasure," "The Mystery of Threshold," "The Initial Effort," "The Meaning of Pain," and "The Secret of Strength." Instead of speculating upon mysteries that lie at the very end of man's destiny, and which cannot be approached by any manner of conjecture, the work very sensibly takes up that which lies next at hand, that which constitutes the first step to be taken if we are ever to take a second one, and teaches us its significance. At the outset we must cope with sensation and learn its nature and meaning. An important teaching of *Light on the Path* has been misread by many. We are not enjoined to kill out sensation, but to "kill out *desire* for sensation," which is something quite different. "Sensation, as we obtain it through the physical body, affords us all that induces us to live in that shape," says this work. The problem is, to extract the meaning which it holds for us. That is what existence is for. "If men will but pause and consider what lessons they have learned from pleasure and pain, much might be guessed of that strange thing which causes these effects."

"The question concerning results seemingly unknowable, that concerning the life beyond the Gates," is presented as one that has been asked throughout the ages, coming at the hour "when the flower of civilization had blown to its full, and when its petals are but slackly held together," the period when man reaches the greatest physical development of his cycle. It is then that in the distance a great glittering is seen, before which many drop their eyes bewildered and dazzled, though now and then one is found brave enough to gaze fixedly on this glittering, and to decipher something of the shape within it. "Poets and philosophers, thinkers and teachers, all those who are the 'elder brothers of the race' — have beheld this sight from time to time, and some among them have recognized in the bewildering glitter the outlines of the Gates of Gold."

Those Gates admit us to the sanctuary of man's own nature, to the place whence his life-power comes, and where he is priest of the shrine of life. It needs but a strong hand to push them open, we are told. "The courage to enter them is the courage to search the recesses of one's own nature without fear and without shame. In the fine part, the essence, the flavor of the man, is found the key which unlocks those great Gates."

The necessity of killing out the sense of separateness is profoundly emphasized as one of the most important factors in this process. We must divest ourselves of the illusions of the material life. "When we desire to speak with those who have tried the Golden Gates and pushed them open, then it is very necessary — in fact it is essential — to discriminate, and not bring into our life the confusions of our sleep. If we do, we are reckoned as madmen, and fall back into the darkness where there is no friend but chaos. This chaos has followed every effort of man that is written in history; after civilization has flowered, the flower falls and dies, and winter and darkness destroy it." In this last sentence is indicated the purpose of civilization. It is the blossoming of a race, with the purpose of producing a certain spiritual fruit; this fruit having ripened, then the degeneration of the great residuum begins, to be worked over and over again in the grand fermenting processes of reincarnation. Our great civilization is now flowering and in this fact we may read the reason for the extraordinary efforts to sow the seed of the Mystic Teachings wherever the mind of man may be ready to receive it.

In the "Mystery of Threshold," we are told that "only a man who has the potentialities in him both of the voluptuary and the stoic has any chance of entering the Golden Gates. He must be capable of testing and valuing to its most delicate fraction every joy existence has to give; and he must be capable of denying himself all pleasure, and that without suffering from the denial."

The fact that the way is different for each individual is finely set forth in "The Initial Effort," in the words that man "may burst the shell that holds him in darkness, tear the veil that hides him from the eternal, at any moment where it is easiest for him to do so; and most often this point will be where he least expects to find it." By this we may see the uselessness of laying down arbitrary laws in the matter.

The meaning of those important words, "All steps are necessary to make up the ladder," finds a wealth of illustration here. These sentences are particularly pregnant: "Spirit is not a gas created by matter, and we cannot create our future by forcibly using one material agent and leaving out the rest. Spirit is the great life on which matter rests, as does the rocky world on the free and fluid ether;

whenever we can break our limitations we find ourselves on that marvellous shore where Wordsworth
once saw the gleam of the gold." Virtue, being of
the material life, man has not the power to carry
it with him, "yet the aroma of his good deeds is a
far sweeter sacrifice than the odor of crime and
cruelty."

"To the one who has lifted the golden latch
the spring of sweet waters, the fountain itself whence
all softness arises, is opened and becomes part of
his heritage. But before this can be reached a heavy
weight has to be lifted from the heart, an iron bar
which holds it down and prevents it from arising
in its strength."

The author here wishes to show that there is
sweetness and light in occultism, and not merely a
wide dry level of dreadful Karma, such as some
Theosophists are prone to dwell on. And this sweetness and light may be reached when we discover
the iron bar and raising it shall permit the heart
to be free. This iron bar is what the Hindus call
"the knot of the heart"! In their scriptures they
talk of unloosing this knot, and say that when that
is accomplished freedom is near. But what is the
iron bar and the knot? is the question we must
answer. It is the astringent power of self — of
egotism — of the idea of separateness. This idea has
many strongholds. It holds its most secret court and
deepest counsels near the far removed depths and

[108]

center of the heart. But it manifests itself first, in that place which is nearest to our ignorant perceptions, where we see it first after beginning the search. When we assault and conquer it there it disappears. It has only retreated to the next row of outworks where for a time it appears not to our sight, and we imagine it killed, while it is laughing at our imaginary conquests and security. Soon again we find it and conquer again, only to have it again retreat. So we must follow it up if we wish to grasp it at last in its final stand just near the "kernel of the heart." There it has become "an iron bar that holds down the heart," and there only can the fight be really won. That disciple is fortunate who is able to sink past all the pretended outer citadels and seize at once this *personal devil* who holds the bar of iron, and there wage the battle. If won there, it is easy to return to the outermost places and take them by capitulation. This is very difficult, for many reasons. It is not a mere juggle of words to speak of this trial. It is a living tangible thing that can be met by any real student. The great difficulty of rushing at once to the center lies in the unimaginable terrors which assault the soul on its short journey there. This being so it is better to begin the battle on the outside in just the way pointed out in this book and *Light on the Path,* by testing experience and learning from it.

In the lines quoted the author attempts to direct

the eyes of a very materialistic age to the fact which
is an accepted one by all true students of occultism,
that the true heart of a man — which is visibly rep-
resented by the muscular heart — is the focus point
for spirit, for knowledge, for power; and that from
that point the converged rays begin to spread out
fan-like, until they embrace the Universe. So it is
the Gate. And it is just at that neutral spot of
concentration that the pillars and the doors are fixed.
It is beyond it that the glorious golden light burns,
and throws up a "burnished glow." We find in
this the same teachings as in the Upanishads. The
latter speaks of "the ether which is within the
heart," and also says that we must pass across
that ether.

"The Meaning of Pain" is considered in a way
which throws a great light on the existence of that
which for ages has puzzled many learned men.
"Pain arouses, softens, breaks, and destroys. Regarded from a sufficiently removed standpoint, it
appears as a medicine, as a knife, as a weapon, as a
poison, in turn. It is an implement, a thing which
is used, evidently. What we desire to discover is,
who is the user; what part of ourselves is it that
demands the presence of this thing so hateful to
the rest?"

The task is, to rise above both pain and pleasure
and unite them to our service. "Pain and pleasure
stand apart and separate, as do the two sexes; and

it is in the merging, the making the two into one, that joy and deep sensation and profound peace are obtained. Where there is neither male nor female, neither pain nor pleasure, there is the god in man dominant, and then is life real."

The following passage can hardly fail to startle many good people: "Destiny, the inevitable, does indeed exist for the race and for the individual; but who can ordain this save the man himself? There is no clew in heaven or earth to the existence of any ordainer other than the man who suffers or enjoys that which is ordained." But can any earnest student of Theosophy deny, or object to this? Is it not a pure statement of the law of Karma? Does it not agree perfectly with the teaching of the Bhagavat-Gita? There is surely no power which sits apart like a judge in court, and fines us or rewards us for this misstep or that merit; it is we who shape, or ordain, our own future.

God is not denied. The seeming paradox that a God exists within each man is made clear when we perceive that our separate existence is an illusion; the physical, which makes us separate individuals, must eventually fall away, leaving each man one with all men, and with God, who is the Infinite.

And the passage which will surely be widely misunderstood is that in "The Secret of Strength." "Religion holds a man back from the path, prevents his stepping forward, for various very plain reasons.

[111]

First, it makes the vital mistake of distinguishing between good and evil. Nature knows no such distinctions." Religion is always man-made. It cannot therefore be the whole truth. It is a good thing for the ordinary and outside man, but surely it will never bring him to the Gates of Gold. If religion be of God how is it that we find that same God in his own works and acts violating the precepts of religion? He kills each man once in life; every day the fierce elements and strange circumstances which he is said to be the author of, bring on famine, cold and innumerable untimely deaths; where then, in The True, can there be any room for such distinctions as right and wrong? The disciple must, as he walks on the path, abide by law and order, but if he pins his faith on any religion whatever he will stop at once, and it makes no matter whether he sets up Mahatmas, Gods, Krishna, Vedas or mysterious acts of grace, each of these will stop him and throw him into a rut from which even heavenly death will not release him. Religion can only teach morals and ethics. It cannot answer the question "what am I?" The Buddhist ascetic holds a fan before his eyes to keep away the sight of objects condemned by his religion. But he thereby gains no knowledge, for that part of him which is affected by the improper sights has to be known by the man himself, and it is by experience alone that the knowledge can be possessed and assimilated.

The book closes gloriously, with some hints that have been much needed. Too many, even of the sincerest students of occultism, have sought to ignore that one-half of their nature, which is here taught to be necessary. Instead of crushing out the animal nature, we have here the high and wise teaching that we must learn to fully understand the animal and subordinate it to the spiritual. "The god in man, degraded, is a thing unspeakable in its infamous power of production. The animal in man, elevated, is a thing unimaginable in its great powers of service and of strength," and we are told that our animal self is a great force, the secret of the old-world magicians, and of the coming race which Lord Lytton foreshadowed. "But this power can only be attained by giving the god the sovereignty. Make your animal ruler over your self, and he will never rule others."

This teaching will be seen to be identical with that of the closing words of *The Idyll of the White Lotus:* "He will learn how to expound spiritual truths, and to enter into the life of his highest self, and he can learn also to hold within him the glory of that higher self, and yet to retain life upon this planet so long as it shall last, if need be; to retain life in the vigor of manhood, till his entire work is completed, and he has taught the three truths to all who look for light."

There are three sentences in the book which

[113]

ought to be imprinted in the reader's mind, and we present them inversely:

"Secreted and hidden in the heart of the world and the heart of man is the light which can illumine all life, the future and the past."

"On the mental steps of a million men Buddha passed through the Gates of Gold; and because a great crowd pressed about the threshold he was able to leave behind him words which prove that those gates will open."

"This is one of the most important factors in the development of man, the recognition — profound and complete recognition — of the law of universal unity and coherence."